# Practicing
## Theological
### Interpretation

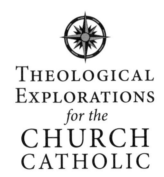

# THEOLOGICAL
# EXPLORATIONS
## *for the*
# CHURCH
# CATHOLIC

# Practicing Theological Interpretation

### Engaging Biblical Texts
### for Faith and Formation

## JOEL B. GREEN

Baker Academic
*a division of Baker Publishing Group*
Grand Rapids, Michigan

© 2011 by Joel B. Green

Published by Baker Academic
a division of Baker Publishing Group
P.O. Box 6287, Grand Rapids, MI 49516-6287
www.bakeracademic.com

Printed in the United States of America

Library of Congress Cataloging-in-Publication Data
Green, Joel B., 1956–
    Practicing theological interpretation : engaging biblical texts for faith and
formation / Joel B. Green.
        p.   cm. — (Theological explorations for the Church Catholic)
    Includes bibliographical references (p.    ) and indexes.
    ISBN 978-0-8010-3963-8 (pbk.)
    1. Bible—Hermeneutics. 2. Bible—Theology. 3. Wesley, John, 1703–1791.
I. Title.
    BS476.G724 2012
    220.601—dc23                                                      2011028360

11   12   13   14   15   16   17        7   6   5   4   3   2   1

In keeping with biblical principles of creation stewardship, Baker Publishing Group advocates the responsible use of our natural resources. As a member of the Green Press Initiative, our company uses recycled paper when possible. The text paper of this book is composed in part of post-consumer waste.

green
press
INITIATIVE

# Contents

# Series Preface

Long before Brian McLaren began speaking about a "generous orthodoxy," John Wesley attempted to carry out his ministry and engage in theological conversations with what he called a "catholic spirit." Although he tried to remain "united by the tenderest and closest ties to one particular congregation"[1] (i.e., Anglicanism) all his life, he also made it clear that he was committed to the orthodox Christianity of the ancient creeds, and his library included books from a variety of theological traditions within the church catholic. We at Nazarene Theological Seminary (NTS) remain committed to the theological tradition associated with Wesley but, like Wesley himself, are very conscious of the generous gifts we have received from a variety of theological traditions. One specific place this happens in the ongoing life of our community is in the public lectures funded by the generosity of various donors. It is from those lectures that the contributions to this series arise.

1. John Wesley, *Sermon 39*, "Catholic Spirit," §III.4, in *Bicentennial Edition of the Works of John Wesley* (Nashville: Abingdon, 1985), 2:79–95. We know, however, that his public ties with Anglicanism were at some points in his life anything but tender and close.

The books in this series are expanded forms of public lectures presented at NTS as installments in two ongoing, endowed lectureships: the Earle Lectures on Biblical Literature and the Grider-Winget Lectures in Theology. The Earle Lecture series is named in honor of the first professor of New Testament at NTS, Ralph Earle. Initiated in 1949 with W. F. Albright for the purpose of "stimulating further research in biblical literature," this series has brought outstanding biblical scholars to NTS, including F. F. Bruce, I. Howard Marshall, Walter Brueggemann, and Richard Hays. The Grider-Winget Lecture series is named in honor of J. Kenneth Grider, longtime professor of theology at NTS, and in memory of Dr. Wilfred L. Winget, a student of Dr. Grider and the son of Mabel Fransen Winget, who founded the series. The lectureship was initiated in 1991 with Thomas Langford for the purpose of "bringing outstanding guest theologians to NTS." Presenters for this lectureship have included Theodore Runyon, Donald Bloesch, and Jürgen Moltmann.

The title of this monograph series indicates how we understand its character and purpose. First, even though the lectureships are geared toward biblical literature *and* systematic theology, we believe that the language of "theological explorations" is as appropriate to an engagement with Scripture as it is to an engagement with contemporary systematic theology. Though it is legitimate to approach at least some biblical texts with nontheological questions, we do not believe that doing so is to approach them *as Scripture*. Old and New Testament texts are not inert containers from which to draw theological insights; they are already witnesses to a serious theological engagement with particular historical, social, and political situations. Hence, biblical texts should be approached *on their own terms* through asking theological questions. Our intent, then, is that this series will be characterized by theological explorations from the fields of biblical studies and systematic theology.

Second, the word "explorations" is appropriate since we ask the lecturers to explore the cutting edge of their current interests and thinking. With the obvious time limitations of three public lectures, even their expanded versions will generally result not in long, detailed monographs but rather in shorter, suggestive treatments of a given topic—that is, explorations.

Finally, with the language of "the church catholic," we intend to convey our hope that these volumes should be *pro ecclesia* in the broadest sense—given by lecturers representing a variety of theological traditions for the benefit of the whole church of Jesus Christ. We at NTS have been generously gifted by those who fund these two lectureships. Our hope and prayer is that this series will become a generous gift to the church catholic, one means of equipping the people of God for participation in the *missio Dei*.

Andy Johnson
Lectures Coordinator
Nazarene Theological Seminary
Kansas City, Missouri

ix

# Acknowledgments

The first three chapters of this book originated as the Earle Lectures on Biblical Literature, presented at Nazarene Theological Seminary, in March 2010. It is a pleasure to record my appreciation to President Ronald Benefiel and Dean Roger Hahn, and to the faculty, staff, and students of NTS for the opportunity to join their community and share in conversation over the period of the lectures. I am especially grateful to Professor Andy Johnson for his hospitality and friendship. For purposes of publication, I have added chapter 4. I want also to record my appreciation to Seth Heringer and Tom Bennett, whose research assistance has been invaluable.

# Abbreviations

| | |
|---|---|
| AB | Anchor Bible |
| ABRL | Anchor Bible Reference Library |
| *ANF* | *Ante-Nicene Fathers.* Edited by Alexander Roberts and James Donaldson. 1885–1887. 10 vols. Repr. Peabody, MA: Hendrickson, 1994. |
| BDAG | Walter Bauer et al. *A Greek-English Lexicon of the New Testament and Other Early Christian Literature.* 3rd ed. Revised and edited by Frederick William Danker. Chicago: University of Chicago Press, 2000. |
| BECNT | Baker Exegetical Commentary on the New Testament |
| BTCB | Brazos Theological Commentary on the Bible |
| *CBQ* | *Catholic Biblical Quarterly* |
| *CBR* | *Currents in Biblical Research* |
| CEB | Common English Bible |
| *CTR* | *Criswell Theological Review* |
| EKKNT | Evangelisch-katholischer Kommentar zum Neuen Testament |
| ET | English translation |
| GBS | Guides to Biblical Scholarship |
| HNTC | Harper's New Testament Commentary |
| HTKNT | Herders theologischer Kommentar zum Neuen Testament |

| | |
|---|---|
| ICC | International Critical Commentary |
| *Int* | *Interpretation* |
| *JBR* | *Journal of Bible and Religion* |
| *JPT* | *Journal of Pentecostal Theology* |
| JPTSup | Journal of Pentecostal Theology: Supplement Series |
| JSNTSup | Journal for the Study of the New Testament: Supplement Series |
| *JTI* | *Journal of Theological Interpretation* |
| LCL | Loeb Classical Library |
| MM | James Hope Moulton and George Milligan. *The Vocabulary of the Greek New Testament: Illustrated from the Papyri and Other Non-Literary Sources.* Grand Rapids: Eerdmans, 1963. |
| MNTC | Moffatt New Testament Commentary |
| NAC | New American Commentary |
| NICNT | New International Commentary on the New Testament |
| NRSV | New Revised Standard Version |
| n.s. | new series |
| OBT | Overtures to Biblical Theology |
| *PRSt* | *Perspectives in Religious Studies* |
| SBLDS | Society of Biblical Literature Dissertation Series |
| SBT | Studies in Biblical Theology |
| *SJT* | *Scottish Journal of Theology* |
| s.s. | second series |
| STI | Studies in Theological Interpretation |
| *TDNT* | *Theological Dictionary of the New Testament.* Edited by Gerhard Kittel and Gerhard Friedrich. Translated by Geoffrey W. Bromiley. 10 vols. Grand Rapids: Eerdmans, 1964–1976. |
| THNTC | Two Horizons New Testament Commentary |
| *ThTo* | *Theology Today* |
| *WTJ* | *Wesley Theological Journal* |

# Introduction

Practically speaking, less than a generation ago in biblical studies the only game in town was historical-critical inquiry of the biblical texts. Yoked with this form of historical investigation of the meaning of biblical texts was its apparently obvious corollary: the yawning chasm that separated biblical studies from theological studies. It is common enough now to hear questions about how best to traverse the distance from "what the biblical text meant" to "what the biblical text might mean today," but this hermeneutic was even more pervasive when I was in seminary and graduate school. If scholars allowed for the possibility that a biblical text might have significance for Christian communities today, it was only after ascertaining the baseline sense of a text in terms of its "original" meaning.

Biblical scholars were tasked with describing what God used to say—or, at least, with what the biblical writers claimed that God said in the past. On this basis, not biblical scholars but theologians, only theologians, could be tasked with making claims about what God might be saying today. Accordingly, attempts by biblical scholars to speak in the present tense of God's words and deeds were, and in many

1

circles today still are, regarded as out of bounds. At best, a biblical scholar might take off the hat of a biblical scholar and put on the hat of, say, a homiletician and, in this different role, dare to speak of God in the present tense.

It is difficult to overstate the breadth and depth of the changes that have occurred in the last two decades with regard to how we engage the biblical materials. The historical-critical paradigm is alive and well, to be sure, but it no longer occupies the same place of taken-for-granted privilege that it did even as recently as the 1980s. John Barton can still proclaim, as he did in 2007, that "the preferred description of biblical criticism [is] the 'historical-critical method.'"[1] In reality, however, the realm of biblical studies supports a veritable smorgasbord of interpretive approaches, interests, and aims, not all of which fit within the rubrics of historical criticism.[2] Among these interpretive interests are approaches that can properly be classified as "theological."

Theological interpretation is not a carefully defined "method." As with other forms of "interested" exegesis, like Latino/Latina or African approaches to biblical studies, theological interpretation is identified more by certain sensibilities and aims. Theological interpretation is identified especially by its self-consciously ecclesial location.[3] In fact, it is not too

1. John Barton, *The Nature of Biblical Criticism* (Louisville: Westminster John Knox, 2007), 31.

2. For examples of this variety, see Joel B. Green, ed., *Hearing the New Testament: Strategies for Interpretation*, 2nd ed. (Grand Rapids: Eerdmans, 2010).

3. Someone might on this basis want to move "theological interpretation" into a side street or even a cul-de-sac, removed from the central boulevard of biblical studies. Such a move would ignore the degree to which historical-critical biblical studies as represented by, for example, Heikki Räisänen (discussed below), is itself *interested*—in Räisänen's case by a commitment to religious pluralism parsed in terms of the priority of "religious experience." This agenda might be at home in the hermeneutics of the late nineteenth century (i.e., in the hermeneutics of Schleiermacher), but it meets its Armageddon in the hermeneutics of Gadamer and Ricoeur, with their respective interests in the contribution of readers, their traditions and their interests.

much to say that no particular methodological commitments will guarantee that a reading of a biblical text exemplifies "theological interpretation." Moreover, so completely have most of us fallen out of the habit of theological exegesis that the category itself defies easy explanation or illustration, with attempts both to describe and to practice theological interpretation characterized by fits and starts—experimentation, really. Nevertheless, the number of resources available to persons desirous of cultivating the old-new practice of theological interpretation of Christian Scripture is growing, and it includes not only introductory texts such as those by Daniel Treier and Stephen Fowl but also the *Dictionary for Theological Interpretation of the Bible*, edited by Kevin Vanhoozer, the *Journal of Theological Interpretation*, and three commentary series.[4]

As we enter the second decade of the twenty-first century, we find ourselves thinking again about forms of reading the Bible that characterized the church throughout most of its history. That is, we find theological interpretation moving into the limelight after hundreds of years of shadowy exile from academic biblical and theological studies. For most of the history of the church, theology itself was primarily an exegetical enterprise, with exegesis taking the form of the homily and theological treatise, along with catechetical lectures and pastoral letters, in which the simultaneity of Scripture—that is, its capacity to speak in the present tense

---

4. Daniel J. Treier, *Introducing Theological Interpretation of Scripture: Recovering a Christian Practice* (Grand Rapids: Baker Academic, 2008); Stephen E. Fowl, *Theological Interpretation of Scripture*, Cascade Companions (Eugene, OR: Cascade Books, 2009); Kevin J. Vanhoozer, ed., *Dictionary for Theological Interpretation of the Bible* (Grand Rapids: Baker Academic, 2005). Commentary series include the Brazos Theological Commentary on the Bible, ed. R. R. Reno (Grand Rapids: Brazos); the Two Horizons New Testament Commentary, ed. Joel B. Green and Max Turner (Grand Rapids: Eerdmans); and the Two Horizons Old Testament Commentary, ed. J. Gordon McConville and Craig Bartholomew (Grand Rapids: Eerdmans). See also the book series Studies in Theological Interpretation (Grand Rapids: Baker Academic) and Journal of Theological Interpretation Supplement Series (Winona Lake, IN: Eisenbrauns).

across time and space—was on prominent display. The rise of various forms of scientific exegesis from the eighteenth century forward has had the general effect of segregating professional biblical studies from the everyday interpretive practices characteristic of the church,[5] and of disconnecting not only biblical scholarship but often the Bible itself from the theological enterprise. The latter chasm is easy enough to spot in claims by biblical scholars that theologians neglect the Bible altogether, collect biblical prooftexts as though they were rare coins or colorful stamps, fail to account for "the context" of a biblical passage, or talk about the Bible without apparently reading it closely; or in claims by theologians that biblical scholars continue to say more and more about less and less, substitute superficial "application" for theological rigor, ignore the theological ramifications of their exegetical judgments, or, with their heightened interest in the historical particularity of biblical texts, effectively remove the Bible from those who might have turned to it as a source or norm for the theological enterprise. Without simply turning the clock backward, as if the rise of biblical studies as a discrete discipline either never happened or served no purpose, theological interpretation nevertheless represents a *ressourcement*, albeit a chastened one, that takes seriously how locating Scripture in relation to the church might remold the craft of critical biblical studies.

A theological hermeneutics of Christian Scripture concerns the role of Scripture in the faith and formation of persons and ecclesial communities. Theological interpretation emphasizes the potentially mutual influence of Scripture and doctrine in theological discourse and, then, the role of Scripture in the self-understanding of the church and in critical reflection on the church's practices. This is biblical interpretation that takes the Bible not only as a historical or literary document but

5. This point is made effectively in Robert Morgan with John Barton, *Biblical Interpretation*, Oxford Bible Series (Oxford: Oxford University Press, 1988).

also as a source of divine revelation and an essential partner in the task of theological reflection.

To push further, theological interpretation is concerned with encountering the God who stands behind and is mediated in Scripture. Theological interpreters recognize that in formal biblical studies the methods of choice have generally focused elsewhere. Some interpreters have attuned their ears to the voice of the reconstructed historical Jesus, to the voices of tradents and then redactors of the biblical materials, or to the voice of the "community" behind the text. Others, especially in recent decades, listen for the voice of the implied author or the narrator, or the voices of other texts heard in the echo chamber of a text. Interpreters might hear the text as an instrument of power, sometimes giving voice to the voiceless, sometimes silencing other voices. In the absence of an "author," interpreters might listen for their own voices, animated by the biblical text. Biblical studies is accustomed to "hearing voices," then, but it has not made a practice of enabling its practitioners to tune their ears to the divine voice—except, in some circles, as a secondary or tertiary task, a derivative step in the hermeneutical process, as though God could speak only after history had spoken. Hear the words of the liturgy:

> This is the Word of the Lord.
> Thanks be to God.

The question, then, is how to hear in the words of Scripture the word of God speaking in the present tense. This *is* (and not simply *was* and/or might somehow *become*) the Word of the Lord.

Critics often complain that persons interested in theological interpretation have spent an inordinate amount of time clearing their methodological throats.[6] It is time to

---

6. For example, Markus Bockmuehl, "The Case against New England Clam Chowder and Other Questions about 'Theological Interpretation'" (paper presented

quit talking about new avenues for engaging the Scriptures, they say. Enough theorizing! It is time to walk the walk, so to speak. These critics fail to take seriously enough the importance of critical theory in this enterprise. It simply is the case that the center of gravity in critical biblical studies has for so long been identified with the historical-critical method that any attempt to escape the strong pull of its gravitational force requires the powerful engines of critical reflection.[7] If biblical studies can simply take for granted that serious readings of the Bible are historical rather than theological, if the categories of evidence are cast in the iron of historical criticism, if the accredited standards of the field are at best ancillary to the theological enterprise and at worse antagonistic to constructive theology, then a certain amount of critical theory and hermeneutical homework is necessary both to demonstrate the problems with the received tradition of biblical studies and to begin constructing an alternative account.

That our present situation merits continued critical reflection is easy enough to illustrate. For example, in a recent and highly publicized opinion piece in *Biblical Archaeology Review*, Ronald S. Hendel, professor of Hebrew Bible and Jewish Studies at the University of California, Berkeley, bid farewell to the Society of Biblical Literature (SBL).[8] According to Hendel, critical biblical studies is occupied with "facts," which do not belong in the same discourse as

at the Annual Meeting of the Society of Biblical Literature, Boston, November 21–25, 2008); idem, "Bible versus Theology: Is 'Theological Interpretation' the Answer?" *Nova et Vetera* 9, no. 1 (2011): 27–47. See, however, the considerable and important throat clearing that Bockmuehl himself undertakes in *Seeing the Word: Refocusing New Testament Study*, STI (Grand Rapids: Baker Academic, 2006).

7. Compare the analogous concern for critical theory in Elizabeth A. Clark, *History, Theory, Text: Historians and the Linguistic Turn* (Cambridge, MA: Harvard University Press, 2004).

8. Ronald S. Hendel, "Farewell to SBL: Faith and Reason in Biblical Studies," *Biblical Archaeology Review* 36, no. 4 (July/August 2010): 28–29. See the follow-up exchange at http://www.sbl-site.org/membership/farewell.aspx (accessed April 8, 2011).

"faith," and, as he sees it, the SBL has given faith-oriented interests so much elbow room that it can no longer be said truthfully that the SBL concerns itself with critical study of the Bible. Hendel's perspective on "scholarship" is hardly idiosyncratic. In fact, his concerns are reminiscent of an earlier essay posted to the *SBL Forum* by Michael Fox of the University of Wisconsin, Madison. Consider these words from his opening paragraph: "In my view, faith-based study has no place in academic scholarship, whether the object of study is the Bible, the Book of Mormon, or Homer. Faith-based study is a different realm of intellectual activity that can dip into Bible scholarship for its own purposes, but cannot contribute to it." He goes on to urge, "Faith-based study of the Bible certainly has its place—in synagogues, churches, and religious schools, where the Bible (and whatever other religious material one gives allegiance to) serves as a normative basis of moral inspiration or spiritual guidance. This kind of study is certainly important, but it is not scholarship."[9]

Let me draw attention to one more case, the concluding paragraph of University of Helsinki professor Heikki Räisänen's important study, *Beyond New Testament Theology*:

> Biblical scholars will soon find themselves at a crossroads. Will they remain guardians of cherished confessional traditions, anxious to provide modern man with whatever normative guidance they still manage to squeeze out of the sacred texts? Or will they follow those pioneering theologians and others congenial to them on their novel paths, fearlessly reflecting on the biblical material from a truly ecumenical, global point of view?[10]

9. Michael V. Fox, "Bible Scholarship and Faith-Based Study: My View," *SBL Forum*, http://sbl-site.org/publications/article.aspx?articleId=490 (accessed April 8, 2011).

10. Heikki Räisänen, *Beyond New Testament Theology: A Story and a Programme*, 2nd ed. (London: SCM, 2000), 209.

In this paragraph, some of Räisänen's scholarly proclivities are clear, but it is also worth noting his concomitant antipathy toward examination of the canonical collection that we call the New Testament, since the choice of these twenty-seven documents reflects later, church-related interests. Study of these documents, along with other early books, should concern itself with the history of early Christian experience, not with theology per se. Such study would benefit humanity as a whole rather than those who look to the New Testament books as the Scripture of the church. Those whose ears are tuned to the right bandwidth may hear in the background the century-old words of William Wrede, who wanted to exorcize from the task and methods of "New Testament theology" both an interest in the "New Testament" per se and a concern with "theology" in order to liberate the discipline of "early Christian history of religion."[11]

Other examples might be given, but perhaps this is enough to remind ourselves that theological interests are not the standard fare in biblical scholarship, that biblical scholars typically have been trained in ways that are at best agnostic and at worst antithetical to theological interpretation, and that the accredited standards of biblical scholarship are commonly articulated in ways that circumvent the interests and needs of the church of Jesus Christ. That scholars such as Hendel and Fox can execute their craft under the assumption that "critical" study excludes the role of theological patterns of faith and life reflects a hermeneutical stance that, for theological interpretation, simply cannot go unexamined. In short, critical reflection on the taken-forgranted hermeneutical commitments of modern scholarship remains necessary.

11. William Wrede, "The Task and Methods of 'New Testament Theology,'" in *The Nature of New Testament Theology: The Contribution of William Wrede and Adolf Schlatter*, ed. and trans. Robert Morgan, SBT s.s. 25 (Naperville, IL: Allenson, 1973 [1897]), 68–116.

On the one hand, then, given the current environment within which biblical studies is practiced, we should not only expect but, indeed, welcome, ongoing critical reflection on the theological and hermeneutical bases for engaging in the work of theological interpretation. On the other hand, it remains true that theological interpreters need to add "showing" to their "telling." It also remains true that the aforementioned theological commentary series have enjoyed mixed success in their capacity to place on exhibition exemplars of the task of theological interpretation.

The chapters that follow together comprise a kind of "show and tell," as I discuss four among the several problems that must be adjudicated if we are to engage in theological interpretation of Scripture. The first question concerns *the relationship between theological exegesis and Christian formation*. I am concerned particularly with the question of what sorts of communities are open and able to hear the words of Scripture as God's word addressed to them. This is the subject of chapter 1. Here I press home my earlier claim that "theological interpretation" is not first a question of method. Instead, I will argue that it is first a question of the role of the reader, and especially the willingness of the readers of biblical texts to present themselves as the addressees of Scripture. Working with the New Testament Letter of James, I claim that the category of "model reader," articulated by the Italian semiologist Umberto Eco, can mark the way forward.

I inquire, second, about the role of history and historical criticism in theological interpretation. Since the late eighteenth century, scholarly work has moved forward under the assumption that history and theology are separate things. (Recall Ronald Hendel's dichotomy: faith versus facts.) Attempts to negotiate the relationship between them typically assume that history and theology belong to different categories—for example, either pitting one against the other as essentially hostile opposites, or, when the two cannot be harmonized, claiming that one can and must trump the other. Working with a well-known text in the Acts of the Apostles and taking seriously recent work in the philosophy of history, I will mark out an alternative approach to this question.

In the third chapter, I will turn to the relationship between exegesis and the Rule of Faith. John Wesley exemplifies in a profound way for those of us in the Wesleyan tradition the importance of the early creeds of the church for reading the Bible theologically.[12] In fact, theological interpretation in any tradition cannot escape the question of the relationship between those ecumenical creeds that define the faith of the church and this canonical collection that we embrace as Scripture. How to work out this relationship becomes pivotal in a case, such as the one I will explore in my third chapter, where, at least on the face of it, the witness of Scripture seems to stand in tension with historic creeds of the church. I refer to the theological anthropology of the Bible, which has it that we are souls (rather than that we possess souls), versus the claim of both the Athanasian Creed and the Chalcedonian Definition of the Faith that Jesus is composed "of a rational soul and human flesh." The relationship of Scripture and the Rule of Faith is thus the topic of chapter 3.

The final chapter takes up in a different way the claim just made in passing: Wesley serves as an exemplar for reading the Bible theologically. Two issues surface here. On the one hand, proponents of theological interpretation have generally identified the need to look to our premodern forebears for guidance in the task of reading Scripture. On the other hand, we live out our lives or engage in biblical interpretation not as "generic Christians" but as followers of Christ embedded in particular faith communities and theological traditions. How does our reading from this

12. For fuller discussion of this, see Joel B. Green, *Reading Scripture as Wesleyans* (Nashville: Abingdon, 2010).

location, theologically and ecclesially defined, shape our engagement with Scripture?

Indeed, how is our theological and ecclesial location shaping our reading of biblical texts without our ever noticing? To what degree are these influences, rather than our exegetical techniques, responsible for differences in our understandings of biblical texts? This issue surfaces even in scholarly study of the historical Jesus, that "scientific" work arguably farthest removed from theological interpretation of Scripture. John Meier notes in the introductory volume to his massive examination of the historical Jesus that "in general, Catholics worship a Catholic Chalcedonian Jesus, Protestants find their hearts strangely warmed by a Protestant Jesus, while Jews, quite naturally, seek to reclaim the Jewishness of Jesus."[13] Similarly, although claiming that his aim was "to be only a historian and exegete," no less a central figure in the so-called Third Quest of the historical Jesus than E. P. Sanders observed, "It is amazing that so many New Testament scholars write books about Jesus in which they discover that he agrees with their own version of Christianity."[14] If this is true in New Testament study defined by its commitment to an alleged scientific objectivity, how much more is it crucial that persons engaged in theological interpretation come to their craft with their theological cards plainly on the table?

In recent years, the tradition that has arguably examined this question most seriously is the Pentecostal tradition—this as a consequence of persons nurtured in the Pentecostal tradition coming to the table of biblical studies rather late, when the rules of the game of critical scholarship had been somewhat loosened, allowing for critical reflection on the Enlightenment project. Casting aside any pretense of coming to Scripture neutrally, these scholars have sought to identify

13. John P. Meier, *A Marginal Jew: Rethinking the Historical Jesus*, vol. 1, *The Roots of the Problem and the Person*, ABRL (New York: Doubleday, 1991), 5.
14. E. P. Sanders, *Jesus and Judaism* (London: SCM, 1985), 330.

both how they are influenced and how they ought to be influenced by their theological and ecclesial commitments in their reading of Scripture.[15] In chapter 4, I do not so much attempt to sketch a full-orbed contemporary Wesleyan theological hermeneutic as to identity some landmark features of such a hermeneutic.

15. See Kenneth J. Archer, *A Pentecostal Hermeneutic for the Twenty-First Century: Spirit, Scripture and Community*, JPTSup 28 (London: T&T Clark, 2004). For earlier proposals, see Kenneth J. Archer, "Pentecostal Hermeneutics: Retrospect and Prospect," *JPT* 8 (1996): 63–81; Arden C. Autry, "Dimensions of Hermeneutics in Pentecostal Focus," *JPT* 3 (1993): 29–50; Robert O. Baker, "Pentecostal Bible Reading: Toward a Model of Reading for the Formation of Christian Affections," *JPT* 7 (1995): 34–48; Richard D. Israel, Daniel E. Albrecht, and Randal G. McNally, "Pentecostals and Hermeneutics: Texts, Rituals and Community," *Pneuma* 15 (1993): 137–61; Jackie David Johns and Cheryl Bridges Johns, "Yielding to the Spirit: A Pentecostal Approach to Group Bible Study," *JPT* 1 (1992): 109–34; Roger Stronstad, "Trends in Pentecostal Hermeneutics," *Paraclete* 22, no. 3 (1998): 1–12; John Christopher Thomas, "Reading the Bible from within Our Traditions: A Pentecostal Hermeneutic as Test Case," in *Between Two Horizons: Spanning New Testament Studies and Systematic Theology*, ed. Joel B. Green and Max Turner (Grand Rapids: Eerdmans, 2000), 108–22.

# 1

## Living Faithfully in Exile

### *Who Reads the Bible Well?*

If today we can talk about any sort of consensus when it comes to study of the Bible, it would be the importance of context. Whether we are thinking of the work of biblical interpretation in the state-supported university, the Christian college, the theological seminary, or the serious Bible study in a college group or adult-education forum, the never-ending mantra is context, context, and context. "A text without a context is little more than a pretext." "Lord, save us from prooftexts!" How? Context, context, and context. This has long been the bread and butter of the work of biblical interpretation.

The question remains, though, of which context. In reality, biblical texts are always read "in context"—that is, in *some* context. Since the mid-1700s, that context has increasingly been identified with the historical setting that first gave rise to the biblical text.

Key to this way of thinking is the presumption that what separates those of us who read the Bible in the early twenty-first century in the United States from the meaning and power of the Bible is a fissure, deep and wide, defined first and foremost in historical terms. The problem we face, we are told, is "the strange world of the Bible." "It is impossible to use electric light and the wireless and to avail ourselves of modern medical and surgical discoveries, and at the same time to believe in the New Testament world of spirits and miracles," Rudolf Bultmann famously wrote over half a century ago.[1] It is hard to read this statement without smiling; most students today would not know a "wireless" if they tripped over one in broad daylight. Moreover, what passed for modern medicine in Bultmann's day would seem quite primitive by contemporary comparison. This is not a new problem, of course. In his note on Jesus' commission to the disciples that they should "cast out devils" (Matt. 10:8), for example, the eighteenth-century cleric John Wesley observed that someone had said that diseases ascribed to the devil in the Gospels "have the very same symptoms with the natural diseases of lunacy, epilepsy, or convulsions," leading to the conclusion "that the devil had no hand in them."[2] What to make of the nexus between the newly emerging "neurology" (the term first appears in 1664)[3] and reports of presenting symptoms and their healing in the Gospels was one of the early problems in ascertaining "the world of the Bible."

1. Rudolf Bultmann, "New Testament and Mythology: The Mythological Element in the Message of the New Testament and the Problem of Its Re-interpretation," in *Kerygma and Myth: A Theological Debate*, by Rudolf Bultmann et al., ed. Hans Werner Bartsch (New York: Harper & Row, 1961), 5.

2. John Wesley, *Explanatory Notes upon the New Testament* (London: Epworth, 1976 [1754]), 53.

3. Thomas Willis, *Cerebri Anatome: Cui accessit Nervorum Descriptio et Usus* (London, 1664), 124; ET in Thomas Willis, *The Anatomy of the Brain and Nerves*, trans. Samuel Pordage, ed. William Feindel, Classics of Medicine Library (Birmingham: McGill-Queens University Press, 1978 [1681]), 123.

With the passing of time and the elevated prominence of historical inquiry, we would learn that the crisis of the relevance of biblical texts is primarily a historical problem. Indeed, it is on this point that critical biblical studies and traditional Christian doctrines of Scripture seem most clearly to be at odds. For biblical studies, the words of the biblical materials are, as it were, historical artifacts; they evidence what once was spoken. For Christian doctrine, the words of the Bible speak in the present tense: God speaks through them today. This poses a basic problem of colossal proportions, encapsulated in modern times by this question: how do we derive "what it means" from "what it meant"? The problem is this negotiation of two historically defined worlds, theirs and ours, captured well in the title of John Stott's classic text on preaching, *Between Two Worlds*.[4] I want to explore an alternative way of construing our work as interpreters of Christian Scripture by focusing on the New Testament Letter of James.

Here is the central question: what does it take to be good readers of James? Were we to prepare a list of credentials, we probably would think of some basic skill with language, an understanding of the historical context within which this book was written—that sort of thing. In the twentieth century, for example, the study of James has swirled around the question of genre, itself a predominantly historical concern. As interesting and important as these skills and this information might be, I want to urge that if we are to read James *as Christian Scripture*, one thing is even more important.

We can think of it like this: Who is the "you" to whom James addresses his letter? Are we willing to be that "you"?

Let me come at this problem from another direction. When we read James, are we reading someone else's mail? This is the basic presumption of critical biblical studies in the modern

4. John R. W. Stott, *Between Two Worlds: The Challenge of Preaching Today* (Grand Rapids: Eerdmans, 1982).

era: James was addressed to people in the first century, whose culture and lives and stories and historical realities are, to put it simply, not ours. But this construal of things is problematic on theological grounds. According to its classical definition, the church is one, holy, apostolic, and catholic. Whatever else it means, this confession has it that there is only one church, global and historical. Were we to take this ecclesial unity seriously, it would reshape our approaches to reading the Bible.

Writing of historical criticism, theologian Robert Jenson has observed that "*the initiating error of standard modern exegesis is that it presumes a sectarian ecclesiology,*" one that fails to acknowledge that "the text we call the Bible was put together in the first place by the same community that now needs to interpret it."[5] A similar perspective was argued by James McClendon, who framed an account of biblical authority in terms of a central theological claim functioning for him as a "hermeneutical motto": "*The present Christian community is the primitive community and the eschatological community.*"[6] For McClendon, it would appear that the fundamental character of the division between the biblical world and our own, or between biblical studies and theological studies, is not historical but rather theological. It has to do with a theological vision, the effect of which is our willingness to regard these biblical texts as our Scripture.

My reference a moment ago to "the strange world of the Bible" was not entirely innocent. I learned this phrase as a theological student in the early 1980s and was taught to think of the New Testament in just these terms on account of its sociohistorical peculiarity. Accordingly, the work of serious biblical studies entailed serious historical work, and serious biblical scholars were to cast themselves first and foremost as historians (not as theologians). Only later did I discover the origin of the phrase in question in the title of a lecture

5. Robert W. Jenson, "The Religious Power of Scripture," *SJT* 52 (1999): 98.
6. James Wm. McClendon Jr., *Systematic Theology*, vol. 1, *Ethics* (Nashville: Abingdon, 1986), 31.

given by Karl Barth in 1916: "The Strange New World within the Bible." What was as surprising as it was fascinating is that "the strange world" to which Barth referred did not have to do fundamentally with human history, human needs, human potential, human practices. This strange world was not a world available to us through archaeology or cultural anthropology or social history. Barth put it this way:

> The Bible tells us not how we should talk with God but what he says to us; not how we find the way to him, but how he has sought and found the way to us; not the right relation in which we must place ourselves to him, but the covenant which he has made with all who are Abraham's spiritual children and which he has sealed once and for all in Jesus Christ. It is this which is within the Bible.[7]

He concludes, "We have found in the Bible a new world, God, God's sovereignty, God's glory, God's incomprehensible love."[8] In the next chapter I will turn again to questions about the status of historical inquiry in biblical studies. Here I simply want to press the point that from the perspective of the interests and practice of theological interpretation, the chasm that first separates us from Scripture is not historical, it is theological.

That is, theological interpretation does not measure the distance between Scripture and ourselves primarily or only in historical terms. For us, the question might become not "How do we span the chasm between 'what it meant' and 'what it means'?" but rather "Why must we assume such a chasm in the first place?"

If the church is one, if the present community of Jesus' followers is the same community to which James addressed these words, if there is only one church through the centuries and

---

7. Karl Barth, "The Strange New World within the Bible," in *The Word of God and the Word of Man*, trans. Douglas Horton (Gloucester, MA: Peter Smith, 1978), 43.

8. Ibid., 45.

across the globe, then this letter has our names written on it. Furthermore—and this is the point—if this letter is to serve as Scripture for us, then we will allow it to tell us who we are.

## The Model Reader

Some will recognize that I have already embarked on the trail of an orientation to reading biblical texts shaped by Umberto Eco's notion of the "model reader." Why the model reader? I could have chosen from among a miscellany of possible readers.[9] Let me mention three examples. Sometimes interpreters speak of, or attempt to reconstruct the identity of, "actual readers." A concern with James's actual readers would accord interpretive privilege to the first reading—or, rather, a series of first readings—by the historical readers of James. However, this is a reading and these are readers to which we have no direct access, with the result that we end up making our best guess on the basis of what the text itself seems to assume or imply of its readers. We simply do not know the identity of those first readers, nor do we know how they might have heard, or received, this letter. As a result, we might more accurately speak not of actual readers but of the text's "authorial audience"—that is, the kind of readers who would have been at home in the sociohistorical context within which the text arose. Also familiar to many interpreters today is the category of the "implied reader," a category developed by Wolfgang Iser.[10] This is the reader marked by the text, the reader whose legs are firmly planted in the structure of the text itself. This reader is a construct of the text, not to be confused with actual readers.

9. For something of the range of possibilities, see Peter J. Rabinowitz, "Reader-Response Theory and Criticism," in *The Johns Hopkins Guide to Literary Theory and Criticism*, ed. Michael Groden and Martin Kreiswirth (Baltimore: Johns Hopkins University Press, 1994), 606–9.

10. Wolfgang Iser, *The Implied Reader: Patterns of Communication in Prose Fiction from Bunyan to Beckett* (Baltimore: Johns Hopkins University Press, 1974).

Why the model reader? My sense is that Eco's understanding of reading takes us in just the right direction if we are interested in an engagement with Scripture that moves us beyond too narrow an interest in the voice or intent of the human author, that moves us beyond the restrictions placed on an implied reader, and that moves us in the direction of according privilege to the role of these texts in divine self-disclosure.

Eco speaks of good reading as the practice of those who are able to deal with texts in the act of interpreting in the same way as the author dealt with them in the act of writing.[11] Such a reader is the precondition for actualizing the potential of a text to engage and transform us, for it is this reader whom the text not only presupposes but also cultivates. This requires that readers enter cooperatively into the discursive dynamic of the text, while leaving open the possibility that the text may be hospitable to other interpretations.

Obviously, this approach eschews an interpretive agenda governed by readerly neutrality, that holy grail of biblical studies in the modern period. Equally obviously, it opens the way for us to develop our concern with the formation of persons and communities who embody and put into play—who perform—Scripture.

My use of the category of model reader does not allow apathy concerning historical questions but recognizes that biblical texts are themselves present to us as cultural products that, then, draw on, actualize, propagate, and/or undermine the context within which they were generated. In the case of reading Scripture, the notion of a model reader also recognizes the contextual location of biblical texts in larger, concentric circles. These include the complex network of intertextual connections that draw later biblical books into

11. See Umberto Eco, *The Role of the Reader: Explorations in the Semiotics of Texts*, Advances in Semiotics (Bloomington: Indiana University Press, 1979), 7–11. For orientation, see also Umberto Eco with Richard Rorty, Jonathan Culler, and Christine Brooke-Rose, *Interpretation and Overinterpretation*, ed. Stefan Collini (Cambridge: Cambridge University Press, 1992).

earlier ones and thereby extend their ongoing influence, canonical relations that enrich the possibilities of interpretive interplay at the same time that they bar readings that fall outside the parameters of the church's "rule," the story of the church's interpretation and embodiment of its Scriptures, as well as other ways of conceiving the ecclesial location of the Scriptures. This includes the contextualization of Scripture in relation to the church's practices of mission and song, baptism and Eucharist, hospitality and prayer, service and proclamation, gathering and scattering.

As model readers generated by this text, we are guarded from too easily colonizing or objectifying the text, instead hearing its own voice from within its own various contextual horizons. At the same time, we remain open to God's challenge of developing those habits of life that make us receptive to God's vision, God's character, and God's project, animating these texts as Scripture and, then, textualized in and emanating from these pages. We come to Scripture with dispositions of risky openness to a reordering of the world, repentance for attitudes of defiance of the grace of God's self-revelation, hospitable to a conversion of our own imagination.

From the standpoint of literary theory, I have urged that we embrace the status of the model reader of these biblical texts. Were we to do so, we would not visit these ancient texts as though they were alien territory. We would not come to them as visitors at all, but rather we would make our home in them even while recognizing that to do so would be to declare ourselves strangers in the world that we presently indwell. We would take on the persona of their addressees, allowing the terms of these texts to address us: to critique, to encourage, to motivate, to instruct, to redirect—that is, to shape us.

### To Whom Is James Addressed?

Who, then, is the "you" to whom the Letter of James is addressed? Listen to the words of James 1:1:

> From James, a servant of God and of the Lord Jesus Christ, to the twelve tribes in the Dispersion. Greetings! (my translation)

In naming his audience, James introduces two categories at once. His reference to the twelve tribes is an eschatological category signifying the end of the ages, marked by the restoration of God's people.[12] His reference to the dispersion points to the exilic life of God's people, awaiting restoration. Here, then, is the paradox of the life of James's model readers: *they are God's restored people, awaiting restoration.* That is, James draws on two competing metaphors: one signifying the restoration of Israel and one signifying the status of Israel scattered among the nations and in need of and awaiting restoration. God has acted decisively to form the eschatological people of God, yet, while awaiting the eschaton, those very people live in a world whose commitments and habits are counter to those of God. The result is that James addresses his letter to people who are not at home, who do not belong, followers of Jesus whose lives are lived on the margins of acceptable society, whose deepest allegiances and dispositions do not line up very well with what matters most in the world within which life is lived.

The truth is, what keeps us from reading James as a letter addressed to us, as our mail, is that it is hard to read. This is because this letter seeks an audience of persons who, on account of declarations of allegiance to the lordship of Jesus Christ, now find themselves living on the margins of society. They are exiles, refugees. They are not at home. They do not belong.

To read James well, then, we will hear already in this opening a most unwelcome description of ourselves. Life in exile—this is not the sort of life most of us want to live. This

---

12. See the discussion in Todd C. Penner, *The Epistle of James and Eschatology: Re-reading an Ancient Christian Letter*, JSNTSup 121 (Sheffield: Sheffield Academic Press, 1996), 181–83.

is not the existence we have chosen for ourselves. Most of us were not parented with the aim of our becoming societal misfits, and most of us have made decisions about education and vocation contrary to such an objective. Consequently, we do not easily find ourselves in a good position to hear the Letter of James *as Christian Scripture*.

Indeed, there is something comforting about reading a letter like James according to the protocols of historical criticism. From the interpretive stance of historical criticism, we can speak neutrally of James's first-century readers. We can read his words dispassionately. These words belong to the first century, not the twenty-first. That was then, this is now. But we are thinking here not about the text simply as an object of interpretation; theological interpretation pushes further in its concern to hear Scripture as a subject in discourse. How does James address the one, holy, apostolic, catholic church?

All of the linguistic skills we might develop, all of the material on historical background we might accumulate, all of the nuance on literary genre—none of this will make up for the basic reality that, as a whole, we do not want to think of ourselves as dwelling on the world's margins. We choose our clothes otherwise. We choose our careers otherwise. We choose our friends otherwise. We do not easily adopt a way of life that assumes or guarantees our minority status in the world. We want to belong. And, therefore, we do not easily hear James as divine word.

The principal problem is not our lack of information about folks in the first century. The issue is theological. What separates us from the biblical text *read as Scripture* is not so much its antiquity as its unhandy, inconvenient claim on our lives. We are not ready to embrace this God. We are not ready to embrace the identity of God's people thus defined. We do not want James to tell us who we are. We are not ready to live in the dispersion.

Life in the dispersion, exiled people—think of the terms that this might bring to mind:[13]

- traumatic dispersal
- expulsion from the homeland
- violent removal
- life on the move—away from taken-for-granted social programs and infrastructure
- assault on, and erosion of, the identity of a people
- movement from the center to the periphery
- loss of social and cultural roots
- separation from the nourishment of family and tradition
- refugees
- loss of self-rule and self-determination

These are some of the common features of the dispersion, and James provides his own list:

- "trials of every kind" (1:2)
- the "testing of your faith" (1:3)
- humiliation (1:9)
- "temptation" (1:12)
- "distress" (1:27)
- "conflicts and disputes" (4:1)
- victims of fraudulent behavior (5:4)
- condemnation and murder (5:6)
- a life of "wandering" (5:19)

13. In fact, "diaspora" (and "exile") refers to a complex of experiences, though the following list includes common motifs. See Robin Cohen, *Global Diasporas: An Introduction*, Global Diasporas (Seattle: University of Washington Press, 1997) (especially table 1.1, "Common features of a diaspora" [p. 26]); Jan Felix Gaertner, ed., *Writing Exile: The Discourse of Displacement in Greco-Roman Antiquity and Beyond*, Mnemosyne: Bibliotheca Classica Batava Supplementum 83 (Leiden: Brill, 2007).

How do we make sense of such a world? What is the role of faith in how we perceive and interpret the meaning of our lives, episodes in our lives, our interaction with others, even world news, in the midst of such a life? James was vitally concerned with these questions. He is fully aware of the struggles that his readers experience in their day-to-day lives. James does not deny the reality of suffering but recognizes that he is addressing persons whose commitments to the lordship of Jesus Christ have led to transformed attitudes and behaviors that locate them squarely in the dispersion. So he works hard to shape both how people find their identity and how they respond in their life situations.

To show how this is so, my plan is to set out two claims, the first preparatory to the second. First, I want to highlight the importance of narrative for the way we make sense of our lives. Second, I want to show how James works to transform the way we see life by locating us in a narrative that is, quite simply, not of this world.

## The Importance of Narrative

I want first to sketch two interrelated observations from the neurosciences about the nature of human formation and knowing that serendipitously prepare us to explore what James is doing in his letter.

### Never-Enough Information

In a fascinating discussion of "the machinery of the cerebral cortex," Christof Koch observes the general deficit of incoming sensory data necessary for an unambiguous interpretation of the object of our perception. This is true from the seemingly more mundane activity of our visual systems to larger-scale hermeneutical concerns, our reflection on and the practices of human understanding. Simply put, we never have enough sensory information for making decisions about negotiating the world around us; nevertheless, those of us with relatively healthy brains make decisions and carry out our lives in the world. How is this possible? Koch observes that our "cortical networks *fill in*." That is, on the basis of our histories and experiences, we fit the information that we have about the present into the patterns of what we have come to expect. Our cortical networks "make their best guess, given the incomplete information. . . . This general principle, expressed colloquially as 'jumping to conclusions,' guides much of human behavior."[14] We see a limousine parked in front of a church on a Saturday afternoon and, without a second's hesitation, imagine a wedding going on inside. Walking near a sports arena, we see a young woman, clearly well over six feet tall, carrying a gym bag, and we wonder which team she plays for. We classify people instantly—up, down, in, or out—based on the color of their teeth, the pigmentation of their skin, the presence of tattoos or accents, or whether they are wearing leather NASCAR jackets. We locate bits and pieces of data in larger frames and interpret them in terms of what we have come to expect.

We can talk about these frames or patterns in various ways. For some philosophers and theologians, we "fill in" in terms of our "imagination." Mark Johnson refers to imagination as "a basic image-schematic capacity for ordering our experience."[15] Garrett Green thinks of imagination as "the paradigmatic faculty, the ability of human beings to recognize in accessible exemplars the constitutive organizing patterns of other, less accessible and more complex objects of cognition."[16] In other words, he suggests, we make sense of "parts" in terms of our prior grasp of "wholes." For its explanatory power, I am

14. Christof Koch, *The Quest for Consciousness: A Neurobiological Approach* (Englewood, CO: Roberts, 2004), 23.

15. Mark Johnson, *The Body in the Mind: The Bodily Basis of Meaning, Imagination, and Reason* (Chicago: University of Chicago Press, 1987), xx.

16. Garrett Green, *Imagining God: Theology and the Religious Imagination* (Grand Rapids: Eerdmans, 1989), 66.

drawn to Owen Flanagan's alternative phrase "conceptual schemes," which are at once "conceptual" (a way of seeing things), "conative" (a set of beliefs and values to which a group and its members are deeply attached), and "action-guiding" (we seek to live according to its terms).[17] To summarize, life events do not come with self-contained and immediately obvious interpretations; we have to conceptualize them, and, in the main, we do so in terms of imaginative structures or conceptual schemes that we implicitly take to be true, normal, and good.

Daniel J. Siegel, codirector of the Mindful Awareness Research Center at UCLA, has recently acknowledged the coercive power of ingrained brain states as they impinge on human responses.[18] He uses the term "enslavement" to describe large-scale dynamics established by earlier experience and embedded in beliefs in the form of patterns of judgments about good and bad, right and wrong. This is not all bad, he notes. "We must make summations, create generalizations, and initiate behaviors based on a limited sampling of incoming data that have been shunted through the filters of these mental models. Our learning brains seek to find the similarities and differences, draw conclusions, and act."[19] Siegel thus suggests the power of our imaginative structures or conceptual patterns for determining how we make sense of what we see and hear, of how we experience the world. Our conceptual patterns are on display in how we evaluate the president's latest speech, how we view young children boarding a plane, or how we make plans for a family reunion. I perceive the world in relation to a network of ever-forming assumptions about my environment and on the basis of a series of well-tested assumptions, shared by others with whom I associate, about "the way the world works."

17. Owen Flanagan, *The Problem of the Soul: Two Visions of Mind and How to Reconcile Them* (New York: Basic Books, 2002), 27–55.

18. Daniel J. Siegel, *The Mindful Brain: Reflection and Attunement in the Cultivation of Well-Being* (New York: Norton, 2007).

19. Ibid., 135.

### Knowing through Narratives

These patterns or schemes are formulated in our minds in terms of narratives or stories. As a result, as cognitive scientist Mark Turner puts it, "*Story* is a basic principle of mind. Most of our experience, our knowledge and our thinking is organized as stories."[20] Indeed, "narrative imagining is our fundamental form of predicting" and our "fundamental cognitive instrument for explanation."[21]

This observation is well established in brain science, especially through the study of persons suffering some form of brain damage. Individuals with lesions to the neural network responsible for the generation of narrative suffer from a diminished capacity to organize their experiences in terms of past, present, and future. As a result, they suffer a loss in their grasp of their own identities. Narrative is so crucial to the formation of one's identity and beliefs that humans will actually fabricate stories in order to give meaning to their present situations. In a collaborative study of "The Neurology of Narrative," Kay Young and Jeffrey Saver observe that "confabulating amnestic individuals offer an unrivaled glimpse at the power of the human impulse to narrative."[22] This observation is deeply rooted in wide-ranging stories about the incredible lengths to which humans will go to make storied sense of what they take to be true.[23]

This is true not only of persons who have suffered brain damage. Most of us have had the experience of failing to see what is plainly in front of us, until we are told what to look for, and we all operate with strong biases grounded in prior

20. Mark Turner, *The Literary Mind: The Origins of Thought and Language* (Oxford: Oxford University Press, 1996), v.

21. Ibid., 20.

22. Kay Young and Jeffrey L. Saver, "The Neurology of Narrative," *SubStance* 30 (2001): 76.

23. See Todd E. Feinberg, *Altered Egos: How the Brain Creates the Self* (Oxford: Oxford University Press, 2001); William Hirstein, *Brain Fiction: Self-Deception and the Riddle of Confabulation* (Cambridge, MA: MIT Press, 2005).

beliefs that lead us sometimes to perceive what is not actually there.[24] Embodied human life performs like a cultural,
neuro-hermeneutical system, locating (and, thus, making
sense of) current realities in relation to our grasp of the past
and expectations of the future; that is, we frame meaning in
narrative terms. "To raise the question of narrative," observes
Hayden White, "is to invite reflection on the very nature of
culture and, possibly, even on the nature of humanity itself."[25]
We will go to great lengths to impose structure on the data
that we receive from our sensory organs, and this structure
comes in the form of the narratives by which we have learned
to pattern the world.

If this is true, then we face critical questions: Which narratives? Which stories? According to what narratives have we
learned (and are we learning) to structure our beliefs about the
world? What are the narratives that pattern the way we think,
feel, believe, and behave? What stories shape our lives and give
us identity? Alternatives abound: "the little engine that could"
(if only it worked hard enough, continued to think positively,
and kept pushing and kept pushing, it could conquer that
mountain); the promise of "unrelenting progress"; "might
makes right"; and so on. If we perceive the world and shape
our identities in relation to the narratives that we construct
and inhabit, then this is a pressing question indeed: by what
stories do I make sense of the world?

Setting out these observations in this way is useful for three
reasons. First, it reminds us of the importance of the narrative
structure of Scripture itself, including the narrative structure
of the gospel. In using the term "narrative structure," I do
not mean that all biblical books are narratives. Obviously,
James is a letter, not a story. Rather, I mean to draw attention

24. See Aaron R. Seitz et al., "Seeing What Is Not There Shows the Costs of
Perceptual Learning," *Proceedings of the National Academy of Sciences* 102,
no. 25 (2005): 9080–85.

25. Hayden White, *The Content of the Form: Narrative Discourse and Historical Representation* (Baltimore: Johns Hopkins University Press, 1987), 1.

to how, as a whole, the Bible narrates the work of God: from Genesis to Revelation, from creation to new creation, with God's mighty acts of redemption, in the exodus from Egypt to the promised land and the new exodus of Jesus' life, death, and resurrection, the center points in God's grand story. It is in this sense that Scripture itself promotes a narrative structure by which to comprehend the world.

Second, this emphasis on narrative draws attention to the importance of the story of Jesus, whether in Matthew or Paul or, indeed, in the whole of the biblical canon, for making sense of the purpose of God. Understanding the coming of Jesus as the midpoint of the great story of God and God's purpose for humanity reminds us that we must interpret God's work in relation to Jesus. It is in Jesus that God's character and aims are most fully revealed.

Third, this emphasis on narrative corroborates what social-scientific investigation has already identified regarding conversion, including Christian conversion: it includes a reordering of life in terms of the grand narrative shared with and recounted by the community of the converted. I learn to tell the story of my life in a new way: "Before, but now!" "I used to think like that, but now I think differently!"[26]

### The Narrative of James's Letter

Here, then, is the question: what narrative is at work as we read James? Actually, James's understanding of the grand narrative of God's work is pretty straightforward. Although he knows the accounts of various Old Testament personages, such as Abraham and Job and Rahab, these do not so much

26. Peter L. Berger and Thomas Luckmann observe, "Everything preceding the alternation is now apprehended as leading toward it . . . , everything following it as flowing from its new reality. This involves a reinterpretation of past biography *in toto*, following the formula 'Then I *thought* . . . now I *know*'" (*The Social Construction of Reality: A Treatise in the Sociology of Knowledge* [New York: Doubleday, 1966], 160).

provide points on the plotline of Scripture but rather prove to be exemplars of faithful life in the present. The grand mural of God's activity for James includes only three major points, which we can map as follows:

Creation → Present Life / Exilic Life → New Creation

On the far left is creation. On the far right is new creation. And the vast middle of James's narrative is life in the present—which is none other than life in exile.

References to creation and new creation in James are minimal but important. This is because images of the beginning and the end are fertile with opportunities to shape the "imagination," to mold one's "basic image-schematic capacity for ordering our experience,"[27] to sculpt the "conceptual schemes" by which one conceptualizes and behaves in the world. They provide the beginning and end by which to make sense of the middle—past and future stakes in the ground by which to take the measure of the present.

The first reference to creation appears in 1:17, in James's reference to "the Father of lights" (ὁ πατὴρ τῶν φώτων, *ho patēr tōn phōtōn*). Consider this phrase in its cotext:

> Don't be misled, my dear brothers and sisters. Every good gift, every perfect gift, comes from above. These gifts come down from the Father, the creator of the heavenly lights, in whose character there is no change at all. He chose to give us birth by his true word, and here is the result: we are like the first crop from the harvest of everything he created. (1:16–18 CEB)

The CEB is particularly helpful here for making clear that James's reference to "the Father of lights" is a reference to creation (see Gen. 1:3, 14–17), and the larger cotext clarifies that James's interest in creation is focused especially on the nature of the creator God. This God does not send temptation

---

27. Johnson, *The Body in the Mind*, xx.

(1:13–15) but gives good things. This God does not waver between giving good things and bad things; his character is consistently oriented toward good things.[28] Just as God creates light, symbolic of what is good (in contrast to darkness), so God is known for his generosity. He gives "without a second thought, without keeping score" (1:5 CEB), and he gives "every good gift, every perfect gift" (1:17 CEB).

The height of God's goodness is realized in his creation of humanity (1:18), an affirmation echoed in a second text, 3:9. Speaking of the tongue, that "restless evil" (3:8), James observes, "With it we both bless the Lord and Father and curse human beings made in God's likeness" (3:9 CEB). James uses the rare word ὁμοίωσις (homoiōsis, "likeness") almost certainly as a way to call to mind the words of the Septuagint of Genesis 1:26–27, according to which God made humanity "according to our image and likeness [ὁμοίωσις]" (my translation).[29] In this way, James grounds human dignity and the call for ethical comportment in creation and, more particularly, in the God who created humans in his likeness.

At the one end of James's "narrative," then, stands creation and, especially, the character of God the creator. This God is the opposite of a wealthy-but-begrudging scrooge or a rich-but-demanding patron. And in the framework of James's rhetoric, this God is the antidote to the temptation among

28. That is, James is not making an ontological statement about God's immutability, as is sometimes assumed by interpreters (e.g., Dan G. McCartney, *James*, BECNT [Grand Rapids: Baker Academic, 2009], 109); in this cotext, as Timothy B. Cargal recognizes, "James has based his arguments not in the divine essence, but in God's will to provide good things for believers (Jas. 1:5, 7a, and βουληθείς in 1:18)." God is not like the double-minded spoken of 1:6–8 but rather "is completely good and desires only good for believers" (*Restoring the Diaspora: Discursive Structure and Purpose in the Epistle of James*, SBLDS 144 [Atlanta: Scholars Press, 1993], 84–85).

29. Sophie Laws, *A Commentary on the Epistle of James*, HNTC (San Francisco: Harper & Row, 1980), 156. Laws notes that in the history of interpretation a distinction sometimes has been made between "image" and "likeness," as in Irenaeus's judgment that "image" referred to the human's fundamental rational nature while "likeness" referred to the human's moral potential, but she observes that James seems to give no indication of such distinctions.

some to turn to the world's wealth or to violence in times of need. Luke Timothy Johnson develops this point helpfully: "If I forget that everything comes as a gift from God (1:17), then I identify what I have with who I am. And I can be more only if I have more. If another has more, then the other is a threat to me, makes me less. Envy, then, moves inexorably toward hostility and murder: I can be more only if I eliminate the other."[30] At work in this case would be a misshapen view of God and God's world, a conceptual pattern that James counters by grounding the past of his theological narrative in the goodness and graciousness of God on display in creation.

References to new creation in James likewise are limited but important. The first two stand in parallel with each other:

Those who stand firm during testing are blessed. They are tried and true. They will receive the life God has promised to those who love him as their reward. (1:12 CEB)

Hasn't God chosen those who are poor by worldly standards to be rich in terms of faith? Hasn't God chosen the poor as heirs of the kingdom he has promised to those who love him? (2:5 CEB)

Note that eschatological vision is grounded in divine promise, and that the parallelism between these texts suggests that, for James, the "kingdom" is to be identified as future life with God. These texts resonate with others in the New Testament. Thus, Revelation 2:10 counsels the church in Smyrna, "Be faithful even to the point of death, and I will give life as your reward" (my translation). And Matthew 5:3 records Jesus as teaching, "Happy are people who are hopeless, because the heavenly kingdom is theirs" (my translation). As in these texts, so James envisions a future reversal of fortune that stands in sharp relief to the present.

---

30. Luke Timothy Johnson, *Brother of Jesus, Friend of God: Studies in the Letter of James* (Grand Rapids: Eerdmans, 2004), 217.

This reversal of fortune is the consequence of divine judgment, a motif that surfaces in James's final chapter:

> Therefore, brothers and sisters, you must be patient as you wait for the coming of the Lord. . . . You also must wait patiently, strengthening your resolve, because the coming of the Lord is near. Don't complain about each other, brothers and sisters, so that you won't be judged. Look! The judge is standing at the door! (5:7–9 CEB)

Again, several traditional motifs surface here, especially the correlation of the return of Christ, marked by the use of the term παρουσία (*parousia*, "presence, coming") in 5:7–8 ("coming of the Lord")[31] and divine judgment, a motif signaled earlier in 4:12: "There is only one lawgiver and judge, and he is able to save and to destroy. But you who judge your neighbor, who are you?" (CEB). The precise identity of the judge is not altogether clear, and cases can be made that James refers either to the Lord Jesus or to God the Father. Does Jesus return in order to judge, or is Jesus' return the precursor to God's judgment? Given Jesus' resurrection to glory and concomitant share in God's identity, it is unclear that a choice is necessary.

James is concerned not with speculation about the end times but rather with the existential situation of his audience, which involved trials, poverty, distress, and oppression. In the context of life in the dispersion, they are to allow testing to blossom in maturity (1:2). If they take matters into their own hands, then they usurp the work of God. So their response is one of faithful resistance, not retaliation, as they live their lives in dependence on God, who will act to set things right. This is the God who will judge the world, reward the faithful, and punish the arrogant who oppress the needy.

---

31. Cf. Matt. 24:3, 27, 37, 39; 1 Cor. 15:23; 1 Thess. 2:19; 3:13; 4:15; 5:23; 2 Thess. 2:1, 8; 2 Pet. 3:4; 1 John 2:28.

By articulating a vision of creation and new creation in this way, James frames life in the present with interpretations of the past and future that:

- remind us of God's character, gracious in his care and provision;
- remind us of the human vocation that derives from our being formed in God's own likeness—a likeness that has not been lost due to sin and still calls us forward into reflecting the holiness and integrity of God himself;
- remind us that the present period of life in the dispersion is not "home";
- remind us that however permanent they may seem, present inequities are not the whole story. The Lord is returning. God will set things right; and
- remind us that although we are formed in God's likeness, we are not God. The work of judgment and vindication belongs to him and him alone. Our efforts to act as though we are God are not only futile but actually comprise that basic sin by which we find ourselves opposing God himself.

Who needs to hear such affirmations and reminders? People in exile. For persons living in the dispersion, issues of identity and boundary maintenance are pivotal. Who are we in relation to them? What is the basis of our constitution as a community? What are our characteristic practices? By what strategies are these maintained? The metaphorical world within which James's model readers dwell is qualified, on the one hand, by the temporal nature of the experience of dispersion in which the people of God are depicted as a journeying people, and on the other hand, by the socioreligious threat confronting a people challenged with the perennial possibility and threat of assimilation and defection ("if any of you wander from the truth" [5:19 CEB]).

James refers to the problem of the present in terms of πειρασμός (*peirasmos*), an ambiguous term that can be translated both as "temptation" (e.g., "Don't lead us into temptation") and as "test" or "trial" (e.g., "Pray that you won't come into the time of trial"). James is concerned with how followers of Christ live between creation and new creation, in the context of present struggle. As a result, already in chapter 1 he lays out a process with one of two possible outcomes. When believers face trials of various kinds, they should respond in the right way, with joy. This is the progression in 1:2–4:

trials → endurance → maturation (or perfection)

However, there is a counterprogression in 1:14–15:

temptation → sin → death

I have just observed that the Greek term for "trial" and "temptation" is the same. The question arises, then, of when is a trial really a temptation (and vice versa). For James, the answer seems clear enough. A challenging life experience can be either a trial or a temptation, depending on the believer's response to it. It is a trial (that leads to maturation) when believers respond to it appropriately, with joy; it is a temptation (that leads to death) when believers respond to it inappropriately, out of their own evil inclinations. In other words, believers cannot blame their outward circumstances for their lack of Christian growth or for failures of faith (nor can they blame God: "No one who is tested should say, 'God is tempting me!'" [1:13 CEB]). The gracious God has given them the wherewithal needed not only for surviving in difficult circumstances but also for flourishing in their faith. Commenting on this progression in James, Wesley himself concluded, "We are therefore to look for the cause of every sin, *in*, not *out of*, ourselves."[32]

32. Wesley, *Explanatory Notes*, 857 (emphasis added).

We see, then, the importance of how one understands or interprets the nature of life in the dispersion. To a remarkable degree, this is a consequence of how one frames the dispersion—and it is here that James sculpts his model readers by locating them, that is, us—on the plotline between creation and new creation.

## Shaping Conceptual Patterns

The narrative that James structures is crucial for locating his audience on the mural of God's agenda and thus providing a context for shaping their imaginative structures. James sculpts his readers in other ways too. Let me mention two. The first involves a conversion in how we know what we know, and the second, closely related, has to do with his emphasis on Jesus.

To a degree often overlooked, James is interested in questions of epistemology—that is, in what we know and how we know what we know. It seems clear that, for James, our response to the temptations and trials of life in the dispersion has to do with what we know and the basis of our knowing. Consider the data:

- δείκνυμι (*deiknymi*), "explain, reveal" (2:18 [2x]; 3:13)
- ἐπίσταμαι (*epistamai*), "know, understand" (4:14)
- ἐπιστήμων (*epistēmōn*), "understanding" (3:13)
- γινώσκω (*ginōskō*), "know" (1:3; 2:20; 5:20)
- ἰδού (*idou*), "see" (3:4, 5; 5:4, 7, 9, 11)
- οἶδα (*oida*), "know, to understand" (1:19; 3:1; 4:4, 17)
- σόφος (*sophos*), "wisdom" (3:13)
- σοφία (*sophia*), "wisdom" (1:5; 3:13, 15, 17)

Although today we often hear that "knowledge is power," in reality, for most of us at least, our brand of "knowing" is anemic, disembodied in comparison to the practical wisdom of which James speaks. For us, knowing is about information;

understanding is about gathering, sorting, and mastering data; and learning is realized in the accumulation of facts. Compare this with James's perspective on wisdom and understanding:

> Are any of you wise and understanding? Show that your actions are good with a humble lifestyle that comes from wisdom. However, if you have bitter jealousy and selfish ambition in your heart, then stop bragging and living in ways that deny the truth. This is not the wisdom that comes from above. Instead, it is from the earth, natural and demonic. For wherever there is jealousy and selfish ambition, there is disorder and everything that is evil. What of the wisdom from above? First, it is pure, and then peaceful, gentle, obedient, filled with mercy and good actions, fair, and genuine. Those who make peace sow the seeds of justice by their peaceful acts. (3:13–18 CEB)

James draws a line between two kinds of wisdom and understanding: one that is earthly and one that has its source in God ("from above"). Moreover, he observes that wisdom and understanding are measured in terms of the forms of life that they inspire. In this sense, wisdom and understanding are fully embodied, not thought experiments or data stored for future use. In addition, wisdom and understanding function like boundary markers, marking out one group of people over against another: one group composed of the world's friends (4:4) and another composed of God's friends (2:23).

If we pursued this line of inquiry more fully, we would begin to construct an answer to the question "What is 'knowing,' as James develops the idea?" Let me offer a tentative summary. For James, "knowing" is (1) a basic of way of orienting oneself in the world that (2) originates either with the gracious God or with a world turned against God, (3) both generates and maintains group identity (coherence and resistance), and (4) is on display in one's practices.

Of course, to acknowledge that there are two kinds of knowing is to underscore James's interest in a wisdom and understanding that come from above—conceptual patterns, that is, that derive from finding our place in the plotline that runs from creation to new creation, with its affirmation both of God's graciousness and God's involvement in bringing about justice in the world. We might call this a "converted wisdom"—a knowing that is the consequence of conversion and reflects the character of "Jesus Christ, the Lord of glory" (2:1). We come, then, to James's emphasis on Jesus.

The challenge here is that James refers to Jesus directly only twice: in 1:1, where he refers to himself as a "servant of God and of the Lord Jesus Christ" (CEB), and 2:1, which presents a challenge for translators. The NRSV, for example, translates, "My brothers and sisters, do you with your acts of favoritism really *believe in our glorious Lord Jesus Christ?*" The italicized phrase contains a genitive construction: πίστις τοῦ κυρίου . . . Ἰησοῦ Χριστοῦ (*pistis tou kyriou . . . Iēsou Christou*). Recent scholarship has pressed for another translation, opting for a subjective genitive, which indicates the "faithfulness of Jesus Christ" (rather than the objective genitive, which indicates "faith in Jesus Christ").[33] This would lead to the translation "My brothers and sisters, in your acts of favoritism you do not share in the faithfulness of Jesus Christ our glorious Lord." Or consider the CEB: "My brothers and sisters, when you show favoritism you deny the faithfulness of our Lord Jesus Christ, who has been resurrected in glory." The point, then, is that Jesus' own faithfulness has become the norm by which to measure all character and all practices. Playing favorites is a game that elevates the wealthy and demotes the poor. This game is based on a set of rules, or conceptual patterns, that equate wealth or high status among humans with divine blessedness. According to the rules of this game, it makes

33. For example, Luke Timothy Johnson, *The Letter of James: A New Translation with Introduction and Commentary*, AB 37A (New York: Doubleday, 1995), 220.

sense to show respect for people who are highly regarded by others and to dishonor those who occupy the lower rungs of society's status ladder. After all, is it not the case that someone's possession of respect and honor, or lack thereof, in this world is a reflection of how God views that person? Stated like this, the game of playing favorites sounds silly, but this has not kept James's readers, past and present, from playing along. In fact, this game stands in contrast with the status of James's readers as documented in the opening verse of the letter: restored by God yet marginal in the world. And this game stands in contrast with the "royal law" found in Leviticus 19:18 and cited in James 2:8: "Love your neighbor as yourself"; thus, "when you show favoritism, you are committing a sin" (2:9 CEB). "Knowing," for James, is on display in "doing," and, especially in chapter 2, our "doing" comes into sharpest expression in the way we behave toward our poorest, our most marginal members.

In addition to these two direct references to Jesus, we should not neglect how James has woven material from Jesus' teachings into his letter. These are only a few of the pertinent examples.

### James and Jesus: Some Parallels

| James | Jesus |
|---|---|
| "But ask in faith, never doubting" (1:6). | "If you have faith and do not doubt" (Matt. 21:21). |
| "Blessed is anyone who endures temptation. Such a one has stood the test and will receive the crown of life" (1:12). | "But the one who endures to the end will be saved" (Matt. 10:22). |
| "But be doers of the word, and not merely hearers who deceive themselves" (1:22). | "But the one who hears and does not act is like a person who built a house on the ground without a foundation" (Luke 6:49 [cf. 8:15; 11:28]). |
| "Has not God chosen the poor in the world to be rich in faith and to be heirs of the kingdom that he has promised to those who love him?" (2:5). | "Blessed are you who are poor, for yours is the kingdom of God" (Luke 6:20). |

| James | Jesus |
|---|---|
| "For judgment will be without mercy to anyone who has shown no mercy; mercy triumphs over judgment" (2:13). | "Blessed are the merciful, for they will receive mercy" (Matt. 5:7). |
| "But he gives all the more grace; therefore it says, 'God opposes the proud, but gives grace to the humble.' . . . Humble yourselves before the Lord, and he will exalt you" (4:6, 10). | "All who exalt themselves will be humbled, and all who humble themselves will be exalted" (Matt. 23:12). |
| "Above all, my beloved, do not swear, either by heaven or by earth or by any other oath, but let your 'Yes' be yes and your 'No' be no, so that you may not fall under condemnation" (5:12). | "But I say to you, Do not swear at all, either by heaven, for it is the throne of God, or by the earth, for it is his footstool, or by Jerusalem, for it is the city of the great King. And do not swear by your head, for you cannot make one hair white or black. Let your word be 'Yes, Yes' or 'No, No'; anything more than this comes from the evil one" (Matt. 5:34–37). |

This brief and incomplete list of examples demonstrates how James has drawn on Jesus' teachings and powerfully illustrates how James wants to ground the lives of his readers in Jesus' message. We may recall the importance of "conceptual schemes"—those imaginative structures by which we make sense of the world around us, which we share with others, and which find expression in our actions. These are embodied in the stories in which we find ourselves, the storylines out of which we live. For James, the story that forms the lives of the faithful is none other than this: the faithfulness of Jesus Christ.

For James, we can do only what we are. And who we are as followers of Christ is the consequence of our being sculpted to reflect in our lives the faithfulness of Jesus Christ, in whom there is no favoritism (2:1). James insists that such faithfulness is on display as faith leads to action, particularly to the present redistribution of resources and practices of hospitality in favor of the neediest among us. In other words, the terms of faithful response are not set by the conventions and standards of the world in which we find ourselves. Were that the case, we would expect James's counsel to take one of the forms more at home in the world, such as passive retreat from the world, apathy toward the poor, or violent resistance against the wealthy. What we find, instead, is a form of nonviolent engagement: putting into play today the standards and conventions of that day, holding loosely to the terms of this world in anticipation of the coming of the Lord, when we will find our true homes in God's kingdom.

## Conclusion

Strangely, during the past 250 years, "the world of the Bible" has been understood primarily in terms of historical context. Historical criticism has assumed and propagated the alien character of ancient people and ancient problems. The effect has not been simply an emphasis on the need to understand what was going on behind the text of a letter such as James. To the contrary, as John Barton articulates it, the effect has been to identify serious study of a letter such as James in historical terms. Every text is read within a context. Accordingly, the context within which James must be read is its own historical context.

I have no desire to pull the rug out from under grappling with James as a product of a particular time and place. Locating James in a particular social setting allows us to take seriously the nature of its interest in exilic life, for example. However, James invites us into a context other than that provided by historical criticism. The strange world of the Bible, for James, cannot be understood merely in historical terms. What is needed is the theological context marked by James's emphasis on creation and new creation as the bookends within which to make sense of life in the dispersion, and, indeed, by James's invitation to identify ourselves as people who, because of our allegiance to Jesus Christ, are genuinely not at home. This is a readerly response grounded in a theological vision, itself grounded in the exemplary faithfulness of Jesus Christ.

Working with the notion of the model reader developed by Umberto Eco, then, I have urged that James wants to shape a reader capable of hearing, of putting into play, his message. This entails nothing less than adopting conceptual patterns promoted by the letter itself. As Garrett Green put its, "Right interpretation depends on right imagination; whether we get things right or not is a function not only of our intelligence and powers of observation but also of the lenses through which we observe."[34] Of course, James might push further, since for him, "our intelligence and powers of observation" are themselves already deeply implicated in "the lenses through which we observe." For him, knowledge is embodied, and our ways of thinking, believing, feeling, and behaving are patterned after a narrative that runs from creation to new creation.

In this way, theological interpretation of Scripture participates in the well-known mantra "context, context, context." But theological interpretation identifies that context especially in theological terms. Theological interpretation inquires whether we are ready to be the "you" to whom James addresses his letter and to be sculpted in terms of this theological vision.

34. Garrett Green, *Theology, Hermeneutics, and Imagination: The Crisis of Interpretation at the End of Modernity* (Cambridge: Cambridge University Press, 2000), 17.

# 2

## Neglecting Widows and Serving the Word?

*"History" and Theological Interpretation*

Theological interpreters generally have mapped the terrain of this reemerging practice in relation to the antipathy of theological interpretation to historical criticism. Thus, it is often observed that, whatever else it might be, theological interpretation is something other than historical criticism. Given the ease with which historical-critical approaches and commitments have cordoned off the theological interests and practices of the church, this is understandable. Caricatures of both theological interpretation and historical criticism have resulted, however, as the one set of practices has sought to define (or even defend) itself over against the other. This often is due to a lack of careful definition of both historical criticism and theological interpretation. In fact, a variety of interpretive approaches can be

43

classified under the rubric of "historical criticism," just as the words "theological interpretation" are used to describe an assortment of interpretive interests and approaches.

Earlier, in the introduction, I identified theological interpretation as not so much a method as a form of "interested" exegesis, determined above all by its ecclesial location and its concern with encountering the God who stands behind and is mediated through the Scriptures of the Old and New Testaments. Accordingly, theological interpretation, as I am using the term, emphasizes the potentially mutual influence of Scripture and doctrine in theological discourse and, then, the role of Scripture in the self-understanding of the church and in critical reflection on the church's practices. This is biblical interpretation that refuses the reduction of the Bible to a disparate collection of historical and/or literary documents, reading it instead as a source of divine revelation and an essential partner in the task of theological reflection.

What of historical criticism? Today, historical criticism encompasses three interpretive agendas:

1. *The reconstruction of past events in order to narrate the story of the past.* This is historical criticism proper, and I will refer to it as "Historical Criticism$_1$." Outside of biblical studies, Historical Criticism$_1$ simply is the work of the historian, and this explains why biblical scholars in the modern era have tended to regard themselves as historians rather than theologians. Historical Criticism$_1$ might take upon itself to retell the history of Israel or the David saga or the life of Jesus in a range of ways that judge differently the historical value of the narratives in the Old and New Testaments. The result of such an agenda is less a reading of the scriptural narratives and more a reconstruction of the histories to which those scriptural texts presume to bear witness.

2. *Excavation of traditional material in order to explain the process from historical events to their textualizing*

*in the biblical materials.* This work includes a range of methods usually developed under the rubric of historical criticism, from historical criticism proper to tradition criticism, form criticism, source criticism, and redaction criticism. I will refer to this as "Historical Criticism$_2$." This might include discussion of the redaction of the Pentateuch; the identification of the contents of the hypothetical document Q, understood by some scholars to have been a source for the authors of the Gospels of Matthew or Luke; or the analysis of traditional material that stands behind Paul's letters (see, e.g., 1 Cor. 11:23–25; 15:3–5).

3. *Study of the historical situation within which the biblical materials were generated, including the sociocultural conventions that they take for granted.* This I will refer to as "Historical Criticism$_3$." It includes a range of interests, such as the ancient economy, the struggles of peasants, the social status of slaves, or the role of purity in ancient Israel.

I claim that theological interpretation has no room for Historical Criticism$_1$, that theological interpretation is interested in Historical Criticism$_2$ only insofar as it might serve rhetorical interests,[1] and that theological interpretation is very much hospitable toward and dependent on Historical Criticism$_3$.

In order to clarify further the target of my concerns with historical criticism, let me go on to identify the philosophical commitments generally identified with Historical Criticism$_1$ and Historical Criticism$_2$, commitments that I will refer to as

1. For example, if Paul draws on traditional material, as he claims in 1 Cor. 15:3–5, then it is worth asking why. What persuasive agenda is served by his grounding his argument in a shared tradition? See further Klaus Berger, *Formgeschichte des Neuen Testaments* (Heidelberg: Quelle & Meyer, 1984); idem, "Rhetorical Criticism, New Form Criticism, and New Testament Hermeneutics," in *Rhetoric and the New Testament: Essays from the 1992 Heidelberg Conference*, ed. Stanley E. Porter and Thomas H. Olbricht, JSNTSup 90 (Sheffield: Sheffield Academic Press, 1993), 390–96.

the "Historical-Critical Paradigm." I refer to the practice of historical investigation grounded in the following presuppositions:

1. History has existed as an object or sequence of objects outside the historian's own thought processes.
2. Historians can know and describe this object or sequence of objects as though they objectively existed.
3. Historians can remove their own interests, whether theological or philosophical or political or social, as they engage in the task of doing history.
4. Historical facts are discovered in a past that exhibits a recognizable structure.
5. The substances of history can be grasped through intellectual efforts, without recourse to the transcendent.[2]

These presuppositions are themselves served by the principles of historical inquiry classically articulated by Ernst Troeltsch (1865–1923). These include:

1. the principle of criticism or doubt, which strips religious inquiry of any claims to unique authority by insisting that its historical claims must be examined with the same method and thoroughness that one might bring to all other historical claims;
2. the principle of analogy, which undermines the possibility of miracles because these are unrepeatable, unique events;
3. the principle of correlation, which explains all events in the world fully in terms of other events in the world—accordingly, God cannot influence or intervene in the world because God is not a material cause.[3]

2. See Elizabeth A. Clark, *History, Theory, Text: Historians and the Linguistic Turn* (Cambridge, MA: Harvard University Press, 2004), 14.

3. Ernst Troeltsch, "Historical and Dogmatic Method in Theology," in *Religion in History*, ed. James Luther Adams and Walter F. Bense (Edinburgh: T&T Clark, 1991), 11–32.

These assumptions and principles I take to be integral to the practice of Historical Criticism$_1$ and Historical Criticism$_2$. They have been foundational to the division between historical inquiry (the facts) and theological reflection (faith) that has long reigned in serious biblical studies in the modern period. Indeed, insofar as these assumptions, principles, and practices focus attention on (the possibility or reconstruction of) events behind the text, rather than the scriptural word itself, and insofar as they exclude talk of God's engagement in the world, I assume that my audience will grant that historical inquiry grounded in these suppositions and principles is no friend to theological interpretation of Scripture. Accordingly, I assume that my audience will understand why I therefore side with Heikki Räisänen in insisting that the Historical-Critical Paradigm cannot be correlated with theological concerns apart from the historical attempt to describe early Christian religion.[4] Of course, given my interest in theological interpretation of Christian Scripture, my audience will also anticipate that my agreement with Räisänen leads me to a path that he does not take. The conclusion that he draws from this judgment is that theological interpretation has no place among historians of the early church, whereas I conclude that the Historical-Critical Paradigm has no place in theological interpretation.

Admittedly, in the wake of late twentieth-century critical theory, the Historical-Critical Paradigm has been met with a veritable phalanx of questions, not least in terms of the reality that historians visualize the past in terms of their own present interests and concerns, rendering quite impossible the value-free neutrality that this brand of historicism requires.[5] Recognition of these problems has not undermined

4. Heikki Räisänen, *Beyond New Testament Theology: A Story and a Programme*, 2nd ed. (London: SCM, 2000).

5. See Clark, *History, Theory, Text*, 9–28; also Peter Novick, *The Noble Dream: The "Objectivity Question" and the American Historical Profession*, Ideas in Context (Cambridge: Cambridge University Press, 1988).

the practice of historical criticism in biblical studies, however. Instead, those committed to this form of academic study of the Bible have continually reasserted the essential character and importance of historical criticism—that is, Historical Criticism$_1$.

Often the alternative to Historical Criticism$_1$ has been articulated in narrative terms, or in narrative-theological terms. The impetus for narrative approaches to theology has been associated especially with George Lindbeck, for whom faith is a culture that shapes our individuality, our experience, and our emotions.[6] Religion, for Lindbeck, is not primarily a collection of true propositions or a deeply personal experience of the transcendent, but rather a language or culture that enables us to characterize the truth and empowers us to experience the holy. Being Christian therefore involves learning the story of Israel and of Jesus so as to interpret and experience the world on its terms. Hence, the Scriptures are essential in shaping the life world of God's people. For Lindbeck, the Scriptures are a "world" that supplies the interpretive framework within which believers seek to live their lives and understand reality.

If Lindbeck stimulated early interest in narrative-theological approaches, he also served as a lightning rod for its critics, particularly with reference to his apparent indifference to the historicity of the biblical story—that is, whether externally referential events compose the biblical narrative. Whether fictional or historical, what mattered most seemed to be the "meaning" provided within and by the narrative. If earlier study of the biblical materials accorded privilege to matters historical at the expense of matters theological, narrative study of the Gospels and Acts reversed things by pressing ahead with theology at the expense of history. That is, what Mark Allan Powell taught us to call "narrative criticism,"[7]

6. See, for example, George A. Lindbeck, *The Nature of Doctrine: Religion and Theology in a Postliberal Age* (Philadelphia: Westminster, 1984).

7. Mark Allan Powell, *What Is Narrative Criticism?* GBS (Minneapolis: Fortress, 1990).

insofar as it was deployed in the service of theological and not only formalist interests,[8] seemed only to perpetuate the problematic and unwarranted dichotomy of history versus theology. Thus, it may not be surprising that in his study *Jesus Remembered*, James Dunn locates his discussion of narrative criticism in a chapter entitled "The Flight from History."[9]

Is it possible to read the Gospels and Acts as narratives without uncoupling historical interests? In an important sense, the answer to this question depends on how those historical interests are defined and their pursuit practiced— hence, my opening concern with a typology of historical criticisms. In the following section I will propose a series of reflections on the nature of historiography (following Hayden White, I refer to historiography as "the narrative representation of historical events")[10] that problematizes any attempt at Historical Criticism$_1$ grounded in the presuppositions composing the Historical-Critical Paradigm. To these reflections on the philosophy of history I would add a single but crucial affirmation that guides theological interpretation: theological interpretation of Christian Scripture concerns itself with interpretation of the biblical texts in their final form, not as they might be reconstructed by means of historical-critical sensibilities (i.e., Historical Criticism$_1$).

To anticipate my argument, the problem is this: in the case of study of the Gospels and Acts, Historical Criticism$_1$ promises what it cannot deliver. This is because those who practice Historical Criticism$_1$ on, say, the Acts of the Apostles,

---

8. That literary approaches need not develop narrative-theological concerns is easily demonstrated. See, for example, the essays by Andrew T. Lincoln, "The Lazarus Story: A Literary Perspective" (pp. 211–32), and Kasper Bro Larsen, "Narrative Docetism: Christology and Storytelling in the Gospel of John" (pp. 346–55), in Richard Bauckham and Carl Mosser, eds., *The Gospel of John and Christian Theology* (Grand Rapids: Eerdmans, 2008).

9. James D. G. Dunn, *Christianity in the Making*, vol. 1, *Jesus Remembered* (Grand Rapids: Eerdmans, 2003), 94.

10. Hayden White, *The Content of the Form: Narrative Discourse and Historical Representation* (Baltimore: Johns Hopkins University Press, 1987).

have as their sources little else other than the narrative of Acts itself. The attempt to recover what actually happened, which is only an alternative way of referring to Historical Criticism$_1$, requires a series of interpretive judgments about the events recounted in the narrative of Acts, which then provide the raw material for a further, competing narrative. But this narrative does not recount for us what really happened, since it too bears the imprint of a series of interpretive judgments that are themselves open to criticism. To put it simply, the lofty aims of Historical Criticism$_1$ deconstruct themselves on account of the subjectivity intrinsic to each stage of historical analysis. The alternative that I champion is a theological interpretation that reads Acts, for example, as a narrative representation of historical events that by definition must focus on the narrative of Acts itself, not on the events to which this narrative is able only partially to bear witness.

## History Is Narration, Not Imitation

Is it possible to read the Gospels and Acts as narratives without uncoupling historical interests? Let me sketch four closely related considerations that together undermine the ongoing dichotomy of history and theology, whether this is parsed as "history *or* theology" or as "history *and* theology," and point to the nature of theological interpretation's interest in history.

First, those responsible for history writing are forever engaged in making choices about what to exclude and include, and how to relate one event to another. This accounts for the two basic, essential, and distinguishing tasks of the historiographer: selectivity and narrativity. Decisions are required, not only for the obvious reason that a record of everything would be impossible to produce but also to escape the democratization of events whereby nothing has significance because everything is of equal consequence. Yet decisions involving valuation are inescapably subjective, oriented as they are toward particular interpretive aims and set within particular chains of cause and effect. Historians are concerned with what they and their communities deem to be significant among the many events that might have been recorded, and with the relationships among the recounted events by which that significance is marked.

Accordingly, a narrative representation of historical events irrepressibly locates events in a web of significance, events that have themselves been chosen with an eye to their significance for that narrative web. Indeed, even the simple act of remembering is itself an exercise in the allocation of meaning, according to subjective determinations, whether conscious or unconscious, of a significance plotted in terms of past, present, and future. If this "significance" is grasped in theological terms, this does not make the consequent narrative any less "historical." In fact, the segregation of history and theology was and is predicated on a dichotomy alien both to premodern thinking and to virtually all religions today. As C. T. McIntire has rightly observed, the separation between faith and fact or sacred and secular runs counter to traditions that hold "the religious as a way of life, and not as something that can be confined to a special private realm or removed from life altogether."[11]

Second, we need a revised perspective on historiography as "mimesis." This is because "memory" of persons and events is being formed long before the historian appears on the scene to take up the twin tasks of research and narration. Oral history represents and shapes the community of memory. History-telling precedes and constrains history-writing. Moreover, memories are in a perpetual state of flux, being surfaced or suppressed, held or lost, in relation to their

11. C. T. McIntire, "Transcending Dichotomies in History and Religion," *History and Theory* 45 (2006): 86. On theological assumptions in historical inquiry more generally, see Murray Rae, *History and Hermeneutics* (London: T&T Clark, 2005); Alan Torrance, "The Lazarus Narrative, Theological History, and Historical Probability," in Bauckham and Mosser, eds., *The Gospel of John and Christian Theology*, 245–62.

perceived importance. Further, "perceived importance" is measured by how an event or situation is understood as the consequence or cause of an event sequence. From one perspective, for example, Jesus' death on a Roman cross has no peculiar significance at all; it is just one in a series of hundreds of such executions. We can easily imagine a late first-century historian writing the history of the empire without mentioning it at all. From another perspective, say, that of the author of Mark's Gospel, Jesus' death marks the end of the ages and so occupies the centerpiece of Mark's narrative representation of historical events.

With these considerations in mind, the pressing interpretive questions become, on the microlevel, "How is this event related causally to that one?" and, on the macrolevel, "What end is served by narrating the story in this way rather than some other?" To raise the importance of telos, however, is to recognize the inherently subjective and, for the theologically minded, the inherently theological nature of the narrative representation of historical events. From even a minimalist perspective, this is because past occurrences shape the parameters within which we visualize and participate in actions and interpret them in meaningful ways.[12]

Thus far, then, we have begun to sketch a view of historiography that cuts against the grain of the Historical-Critical Paradigm. History writing is always more and less than the past—more because historiography locates events in a web of significance that gives them an importance that they do not inherently possess, and less because historiography is by its nature selective in its choices of what to recount. David Lowenthal summarizes these concerns with three telling observations: (1) no historical account can recover the totality of the past as it really was, because of its virtual infinity; (2) no historical account can cover the past as it was, since the

12. See Steven G. Smith, "Historical Meaningfulness in Shared Action," *History and Theory* 48 (2009): 1–19.

past is made up of events and situations, not accounts; and (3) no historical account can escape the subjectivity inherent in the choices of what and how to remember.[13] Against the Historical-Critical Paradigm, then, we must recognize with Brian Stock that "historical writing does not treat reality; it treats the interpreter's relation to it."[14] The work of the historian is never simply "retrieval," for the modernist historian's aspirations to objectivity falter at the recognition that the historian's craft is exercised in selectivity (what to include) and narrativity (how to order events in a web of cause and effect).[15]

I promised to sketch four considerations that together undermine the ongoing dichotomy of history and theology. The third recognizes that the Gospels and Acts are cultural products; that is, they are narratives that speak both out of and over against the worlds within which they were written. They participate in, legitimate, perpetuate, and criticize the worlds within which they were generated. As Stephen Greenblatt has observed, texts exist in a relationship of constraint and mobility with their cultural contexts, as authors assemble and shape the forces of their worlds in fresh ways that both draw on and point beyond those cultural elements.[16] This means that narratives such as the Gospels and Acts perform like structures for the accumulation, transformation, representation, and communication of the social energies and practices integral to their worlds ("constraint") but also that

13. David Lowenthal, *The Past Is a Foreign Country* (Cambridge: Cambridge University Press, 1985), 214–18.

14. Brian Stock, *Listening for the Text: On the Uses of the Past*, Parallax Re-Visions of Culture and Society (Baltimore: Johns Hopkins University Press, 1990), 80.

15. This recognition in contemporary philosophy of history is deeply indebted to the work of Hayden White, especially *Content of the Form*. For an assessment of White's influence, see Richard T. Vann et al., "Hayden White: Twenty-Five Years On," *History and Theory* 37 (1998): 143–93.

16. See Stephen Greenblatt, "Culture," in *Critical Terms for Literary Study*, ed. Frank Lentricchia and Thomas McLaughlin (Chicago: University of Chicago Press, 1990), 225–32.

these narratives have the capacity to break their worlds' social boundaries in order to reinterpret accepted conventions, to critique social norms, and to visualize an alternative universe ("mobility"). Indeed, narratives have ongoing significance in part because of their capacity to speak beyond the limitations of their own historical particularity. Yet, as "cultural products," the fullness of their voice is shaped by that very particularity.

With this third consideration, then, we find a strong case for Historical Criticism$_3$ and, pedagogically, for refusing the way modern education often segregates the study of history from the study of literature, and both from the study of theology. Taking seriously this aspect of the "historicity" of Acts, for example, allows us a sharper image of how Luke might have pursued the task of shaping the identity of a people through shaping his narrative at the same time that it militates against our impulses toward domesticating this narrative by locating it within our own cultural commitments, as though they embodied and authorized our cherished dispositions.

If the first two considerations counter the segregation of history and theology posited by Historical Criticism$_1$ and Historical Criticism$_2$, this third consideration demonstrates the importance of Historical Criticism$_3$ for the enterprise of theological interpretation. Historical Criticism$_3$, or study of the historical situation within which the biblical materials were generated, including the sociocultural conventions that they take for granted, counters whatever tendencies we might have toward a docetic reading of the Gospels and Acts, as though they concerned themselves merely with ethereal issues, as though our reading of them might fail to account seriously for the central affirmation that the Logos became flesh and dwelled among us. By reminding us of the text's own status as a cultural product, Historical Criticism$_3$ protects the text from our tendencies to recruit its words and phrases to our own ends. And from the standpoint of pragmatics, that area of linguistics that studies how context contributes to meaning, Historical Criticism₃ reminds us that entire patterns of behavior and well-known social scripts can be signaled by a few words in the text; in other words, Historical Criticism₃ reminds us that texts are more than words on the page. From this vantage point, then, a fulsome grasp of the social, religious, cultural complex within which Acts was produced is informative, not so that we might trap Acts within its historical world and not because Acts (or any other text) gives us uninterpreted access to that world, but so that we can see how Acts embraces and undermines its world as it invites its audience to discern and participate in God's restorative agenda.

The fourth and final consideration is that the Gospels and Acts, as with narratives more generally, have intended effects. Narrative is not only story but also action—"the telling of a story by someone to someone on some occasion for some purpose," as James Phelan puts it.[17] Of course, in making this claim, I am departing perspectives on historical study and history-writing deeply (if often unconsciously) indebted to a philosophy of history motivated by a desire to emulate the investigative commitments and techniques of the natural sciences. And I am recognizing that history-writing is to an important degree always interested in the present, that history-writing concerns itself not with objective retrieval of the past but rather with the benefits of the past for the present. History-writing is never conducted in a vacuum of relevance; it serves agendas such as validation of a people or institution (especially through tracing continuity with the past), identity formation, and pedagogy.[18]

We must take seriously, then, the evangelists' persuasive art, particularly with regard to what they have chosen to include, how they have ordered their material, and into what plotline they have inscribed the whole. Like that of any historiographer

17. James Phelan, *Narrative as Rhetoric: Technique, Audiences, Ethics, Ideology* (Columbus: Ohio State University Press, 1996), 8.
18. See Lowenthal, *The Past Is a Foreign Country.*

or biographer, Luke's work, for example, presumes not only the availability of "facts" but also a storyline into which his narrative is inscribed. This storyline includes a beginning and an end, expectations and presumptions, and these tacitly guide the actual narrativizing process.

In short, for us, history-writing is not an add-on to the theological task, nor is theology an add-on to the work of historiography. Although one might wish to speak heuristically of Luke's or Matthew's theological agenda or historical interests or literary artistry, these are not "parts" of a Lukan or Matthean enterprise. A narrative such as Mark's is not molecular, divisible into three parts history, two parts theology, and one part literary artistry. It simply is a theologically determined narrative representation of historical events.

## Acts 6:1–7: Neglecting Widows and Serving the Word?

To put on display the perspective that I have been sketching, I now turn to an examination of Acts 6:1–7. This may seem to be an odd choice for an exercise in theological interpretation. Theologians have not employed this textual unit in their discussions of the triune nature of God, for example, or of their pneumatology, anthropology, or eschatology. Why not turn elsewhere in Acts to such low-hanging theological fruit as the potential of, say, Acts 2:33, for reflecting on a Lukan divine Christology? Why not trace the many references to God's purpose and plan in the book of Acts, so as to warrant theological reflection on the "divine attributes"?

I am drawn to this text for two reasons, both having to do with interpretive assessments of this passage in recent study. First, it has been common to think of the problem addressed by this text in predominantly "practical" terms. According to this reading, church growth has resulted in an issue related to routines and organization; parsed in this way, the church's practical problem demands and receives a different organizational structure. I will show that this reading of Acts 6:1–7 is problematic for its reductionism and that both the problem and solution that Luke recounts are profoundly theological. This text is not (simply) about too many people and too little food; it is about God and, then, the nature of the good news itself. Second, although this pericope has attracted relatively little attention from practitioners of Historical Criticism$_1$ (i.e., the reconstruction of historical events in order to narrate the past) or Historical Criticism$_2$ (i.e., excavation of traditional material in order to explain the process from historical events to their textualizing in the biblical materials), two recent studies, motivated by perceived lack of clarity on Luke's part, have attempted to get behind Luke's account in order to renarrate what was really going on. I will show that these readings fail to take seriously the coherence of Luke's account in its present form within the narrative of Luke-Acts.

I begin by citing the text of Acts 6:1–7 itself:

Now during those days, when the disciples were increasing in number, the Hellenists complained against the Hebrews because their widows were being neglected in the daily distribution of food. And the twelve called together the whole community of the disciples and said, "It is not right that we should neglect the word of God in order to wait on tables. Therefore, friends, select from among yourselves seven men of good standing, full of the Spirit and of wisdom, whom we may appoint to this task, while we, for our part, will devote ourselves to prayer and to serving the word."

What they said pleased the whole community, and they chose Stephen, a man full of faith and the Holy Spirit, together with Philip, Prochorus, Nicanor, Timon, Parmenas, and Nicolaus, a proselyte of Antioch. They had these men stand before the apostles, who prayed and laid their hands on them.

The word of God continued to spread; the number of the disciples increased greatly in Jerusalem, and a great many of the priests became obedient to the faith.

A survey of both older and several more recent commentaries reveals little interest in questioning the basic historical outline of Luke's account of the resolution of the problem that surfaced as a consequence of the Jerusalem community's neglect of its Hellenist widows,[19] though a few attempts have been made to discern behind-the-story evidence of pre-Lukan tradition.[20] The question of the identity of the Hellenists and Hebrews has spawned a longstanding scholarly discussion,[21] of course, along with the question of whether Luke has downplayed the nature and extent of the division that he reports. Moreover, some readers have worried over the nature of the "poor relief" envisioned here.[22] The account as a whole, however, often has been taken more or less at face value as students of Acts quickly moved on to the many questions raised by the material about Stephen beginning in 6:8. Two recent studies have focused their historical concerns more

19. For example, Richard Belward Rackham, *The Acts of the Apostles: An Exposition* (London: Methuen, 1906), 81–87; F. J. Foakes-Jackson, *The Acts of the Apostles*, MNTC (London: Hodder & Stoughton, 1931); Hans Conzelmann, *Acts of the Apostles*, Hermeneia (Philadelphia: Fortress, 1987), 44–46; F. F. Bruce, *The Book of Acts*, rev. ed., NICNT (Grand Rapids: Eerdmans, 1988); John B. Polhill, *Acts*, NAC (Nashville: Broadman, 1992), 178–80; C. K. Barrett, *A Critical and Exegetical Commentary on the Acts of the Apostles*, vol. 3, ICC (Edinburgh: T&T Clark, 1994), 302–17; Joseph A. Fitzmyer, *The Acts of the Apostles: A New Translation with Introduction and Commentary*, AB 31 (New York: Doubleday, 1998), 344. For this section I have adapted material from my essay "Neglecting Widows and Serving the Word? Acts 6:1–7 as a Test Case for a Missional Hermeneutic," in *Jesus Christ, Lord and Savior*, ed. Jon Laansma, Grant Osborne, and Ray Van Neste (Carlisle, UK: Paternoster; Eugene, OR: Wipf & Stock, forthcoming).

20. For example, Gerhard Schneider, *Die Apostelgeschichte*, vol. 1, HTKNT 5 (Freiburg: Herder, 1980), 420–22; Gerd Lüdemann, *Early Christianity according to the Traditions in Acts: A Commentary*, trans. John Bowden (Minneapolis: Fortress, 1989), 73–79; Rudolf Pesch, *Die Apostelgeschichte*, vol. 1, EKKNT 5 (Zürich: Benziger; Neukirchen-Vluyn: Neukirchener Verlag, 1986), 226.

21. The literature is voluminous. See the monograph by Craig C. Hill, *Hellenists and Hebrews: Reappraising Division within the Earliest Church* (Minneapolis: Fortress, 1992).

22. On the question of "poor relief," see Ernst Haenchen, *The Acts of the Apostles*, trans. Bernard Noble and Gerald Shinn (Oxford: Blackwell, 1971), 261–62; Lüdemann, *Early Christianity*, 74–76.

narrowly, however, offering different assessments of certain key aspects of the story behind Luke's narrative.

Among the historical issues on which he focuses, Richard Pervo notices that the resolution offered in this account immediately deconstructs itself, since the seven chosen for "serving tables" appear rather as missionaries. As Henry Cadbury had recognized long before, "It is not clear . . . why men chosen to allow the Twelve to preach rather than to 'serve tables' appear later only as preachers and evangelists."[23] The problem, Pervo asserts, is one of Luke's own making, since he would have been the one to introduce the business of food distribution into the tradition of the seven. What is more, Luke's scene is anachronistic; assuming an identifiable body of widows and a group of subordinate ministers, it is reminiscent not so much of the early church but of the organizational structures of the Pastoral Epistles and Polycarp. For him, Acts portrays the widows functioning as a group that complains about the treatment they have received.[24]

In her book *Of Widows and Meals*, Reta Halteman Finger attempts a reconstruction of the situation behind Acts 6:1–7. Reading Luke's account against the background of 2:42–47, she postulates that shared faith in Jesus has generated a community of believers who shared daily meals; accordingly, the daily "service" (διακονία, *diakonia*) in 6:1–6 is nothing other than the daily table service for which widows had essential roles in the work of food preparation and distribution. The disruption that Luke envisions may have occurred because the Hebraic widows received more honor than the Hellenist widows in the organization, preparation, and serving of the daily meal. The decision to appoint a group of men to oversee

23. Henry J. Cadbury, "Note VII: The Hellenists," in *The Beginnings of Christianity*, Part 1: *The Acts of the Apostles*, vol. 5, *Additional Notes to the Commentary*, ed. Kirsopp Lake and Henry J. Cadbury (Grand Rapids: Baker, 1933), 62.

24. Richard I. Pervo, *Dating Acts: Between the Evangelists and the Apologists* (Santa Rosa, CA: Polebridge, 2006), 219; idem, *Acts: A Commentary*, Hermeneia (Minneapolis: Fortress, 2009), 151–63.

the daily meals could have been either to quell the quarreling widows or to extend Jesus' directive to male leaders that they serve others at table.[25]

Unfortunately, in both instances we find historical reconstruction rushing ahead at the expense of historical narrative. For example, Pervo assumes what is not in evidence: the widows compose a group sufficiently organized to lodge a complaint. Instead, Acts portrays a complaint registered on behalf of certain widows, not registered by the widows themselves and certainly not by widows functioning implicitly as a kind of pressure group. Finger envisions widows preparing food rather than receiving it (or not) and focuses on widows quarreling with one another rather than on the situation of Hellenist widows against whom a disservice was being perpetrated.[26] Her approach to the social history behind the account in Acts seems less indebted to the narrative of Acts than to practices among Anabaptists like herself. Of course, this would not be the first time that an interpreter had looked to 6:1–7 through the lens of later ecclesial practices, as the traditional tendency to find in this text either a general model for leaders to delegate their responsibilities or a specific grounding for the ordination of subleaders known as "deacons" demonstrates.[27] Reconstructions like this may be warranted by certain kinds of historical approaches, but not by the sort of approach that I have sketched, and certainly not before the possibility for reading this material as a coherent narrative representation of historical events provided by the text itself has been fully explored.

We must recognize at the outset that, contrary to the view of a number of interpreters, the problem that Luke presents

25. Reta Halteman Finger, *Of Widows and Meals: Communal Meals in the Book of Acts* (Grand Rapids: Eerdmans, 2007), esp. 246–75.

26. Pivotal for my reading is the use in Acts 6:1 of παραθεωρέω—the act of failing to account for someone or something worth acknowledging, typically with a bad result, so that this failure puts the person guilty of overlooking in a bad light (e.g., Diodorus Siculus, *Bibliotheca historica* 40.5; Dionysius, *De Isaeo* 18; cf. MM 483; BDAG 763–64).

27. See Jaroslav Pelikan, *Acts*, BTCB (Grand Rapids: Brazos, 2005), 91–93.

cannot be understood reductively as a "practical" one.[28] Of course, it is true that this textual unit is enclosed by dual references to the growth of the church (πληθύνω, *plēthynō*, "increase" [vv. 1, 7]), so that the dilemma recounted might be understood as having been precipitated by the expanding numbers of disciples. Five considerations speak against this view, however.

First, just as Luke's repeated emphasis on the unity of the believers is theologically grounded, so we should anticipate the introduction of any dissension likewise to be theologically grounded. The term with which the narrator has often captured the situation of the disciples is ὁμοθυμαδόν (*homothymadon*), "with one accord," used of the followers of Christ in 1:14; 2:46; 4:24; 5:12; 15:25. Thus far in Acts, then, Luke has used the term in 1:14, where the disciples are defined by their tenacious orientation toward a common aim, single-minded in their solidarity, giving themselves to prayer; 2:46, where the disciples are "persisting in their unity in the temple" (my translation); in 4:24, where Luke declares their solidarity over against their detractors and, again, associates their unity with a community-defining practice: prayer; and finally in 5:12, where the betrayal of community dispositions by Ananias and Sapphira is set in opposition to the disciples' oneness. We may add to this the phrase ἐπὶ τὸ αὐτό (*epi to auto*, "together") in 1:15; 2:1, 44, 47, which Luke uses to underscore the oneness of this company of believers both as a consequence of their obedience to Jesus and as an expression of the Spirit's generative work. The introduction of dissension with the community in 6:1, then, is startling not only because it disrupts the thus-far persistent portrait of the believers' extraordinary solidarity but also because it raises questions theologically about what has gone amiss.

28. For example, F. F. Bruce states, "It was over a practical issue, and not over a matter of theological importance, that disagreement became acute" (*Acts*, 120).

Second, just as Luke has demonstrated that the economic *koinonia* characteristic of the Jerusalem believers is the Spirit's work and an expression of the unity of those who together call on the name of the Lord Jesus, so this failure of that same economic *koinonia* must be read as a disruption of the Spirit's work. Both of the summaries whereby Luke pictures the economic *koinonia* of the community of believers follow immediately, sequentially and generatively, from the outpouring of the Holy Spirit (2:1–41 → 2:42–47; 4:31 → 4:32–35),[29] the consequence of which, ultimately, is that there were "no needy persons among them" (4:34 CEB). Although it makes good sense to characterize the community of goods that Luke reports in terms borrowed from economic anthropology, as "generalized reciprocity,"[30] it cannot be overlooked that this is the sort of economic exchange expressive among close kin, and that the "family" of believers that Luke presents are kin in theological and not merely sociological (and certainly not biological) terms. Had not Jesus redefined family when he said, "My mother and my brothers are those who hear the word of God and do it" (Luke 8:21 [cf. 3:7–14])? What action or situation has caused a community among whom there were no needy persons now to have this cadre of such persons? How could such need have arisen within the community apart from a failure of the community in terms of its appropriation of the Spirit's generative work in their midst?

Third, it should not escape our notice that rather than reporting that "some widows" had been overlooked, or that some widows from among the Hellenists and some from the Hebrews had been overlooked, Luke has it only that the Hellenist widows were slighted. Were this merely a practical

---

29. See Matthias Wenk, *Community-Forming Power: The Socio-Ethical Role of the Spirit in Luke-Acts*, JPTSup 19 (Sheffield: Sheffield Academic Press, 2000), 259–73. Wenk works primarily with Acts 2:42–47, but an analogous case for a cause-and-effect relationship between the outpouring of the Spirit and economic *koinonia* can be made with 4:23–35.

30. See Marshall Sahlins, *Stone Age Economics* (London: Routledge, 1972), 193–94.

problem arising from too many people and too little food, on the basis of probability theory would we not have anticipated the neglect of Hebrew widows as well as Hellenist ones?

Fourth, from within the biblical tradition that Luke embraces, to neglect widows *at all* is offensive theologically. Together with the alien and the orphan, the situation of the widow is synecdoche in Israel's Scriptures for the plight of the vulnerable and dispossessed who are afforded explicit protection under the law (e.g., Exod. 22:22; Deut. 10:18). Indeed, in the Psalms we read that God is the "father of the fatherless and protector of widows" (68:5; cf. 146:9). For Luke-Acts, widows are models of faithfulness to God on the one hand, and of poverty and vulnerability on the other; and they are those to whom the good news is directed (e.g., Luke 2:36–38; 4:25–26; 7:11–17; 20:45–21:4). Joseph Tyson's summary is as apt as it is economic:

> In Luke-Acts, widowhood means grief, poverty, vulnerability, and piety. The exclusion of widows from the common meal would, therefore, appear as an act of extreme cruelty and impiety, but also as a condition that underlined the urgent need for a solution. The reader should recognize immediately that here is an intolerable situation, one which can have only one solution: the widows must not be excluded.[31]

For widows to be overlooked in this way, then, signals a theological (not just a practical) failure within the community.

Fifth, irrespective of scholarly speculation regarding the identity of the Hellenists and Hebrews more generally, for Luke they obviously represent different sides in a dispute.[32] In

31. Joseph B. Tyson, "Acts 6:1–7 and Dietary Regulations in Early Christianity," *PRSt* 10 (1983): 158. See also F. Scott Spencer, "Neglected Widows in Acts 6:1–7," *CBQ* 56 (1994): 715–33.

32. Indeed, Joseph T. Lienhard urges that the actual identity of the Hellenists and Hebrews is less important to Luke's presentation than the mere fact that there is dissension ("Acts 6:1–6: A Redactional View," *CBQ* 37 [1975]: 231). The larger question concerns the basis on which one might accord privilege to reconstructions

Acts, Ἑβραῖος (*Hebraios*) refers to Aramaic-speaking Jews.[33] Luke uses Ἑλληνιστής (*Hellēnistēs*) in 6:1; 9:29, in both instances to refer to Greek-speaking Jews within Jerusalem. That is, he uses the term where such a distinction makes sense: outside a city or region whose majority population spoke Aramaic, there would be no need to qualify Jews as Greek speaking.[34] Given the focus of the present textual unit on "disciples" (6:1), we should think of two different sets of Christ followers: Greek-speaking Jews and Aramaic-speaking Jews. As the CEB has it, "Greek-speaking disciples accused the Aramaic-speaking disciples."

Of course, even this is a misnomer, since it is hard to imagine Aramaic-speaking Jews in Jerusalem who were not able also to traffic in Greek—an observation that presses for greater clarity.[35] First, we should think of these two groups as characterized by their dominant language, Greek and Aramaic, respectively, leaving open the probability of additional language competencies. Second, we cannot think merely in terms of linguistic choice, since identification of dominant language necessarily involves long-term formation and affiliations with respect to cultural (and, therefore, religious) identification. In 2 Maccabees 7:8, 21; 12:37; 15:29, for example, speaking in the ancestral language was integral to boundary maintenance when Jewish identity was threatened. Speech assumes but also constructs community, with language and language choices being both a product of and integral to the

---

of the Hellenists based on minimal textual evidence outside Acts, over against the portrait in Luke's narrative. He is theologically motivated, but other sources are not?

33. Note the pattern in 21:40; 22:2; 26:14. See Martin Hengel, "Between Jesus and Paul: The 'Hellenists,' the 'Seven' and Stephen," in *Between Jesus and Paul: Studies in the Earliest History of Christianity*, trans. John Bowden (Philadelphia: Fortress, 1983), 9–10.

34. Luke may use the term in 11:20, but the text is disputed. Ἕλληνας is read by 𝔓⁷⁴ ℵ² A D*. BDAG specifies a Ἑλληνιστής as "a Greek-speaking Israelite in contrast to one speaking a Semitic language" (p. 319).

35. For what follows, I am dependent on the theory of linguistic pragmatics sketched in Alessandro Duranti, *Linguistic Anthropology*, Cambridge Textbooks in Linguistics (Cambridge: Cambridge University Press, 1997).

ongoing production of social relations. In other words, however else we might parse the boundaries between Hellenists
and Hebrews in 6:1, we cannot reduce the controversy to
differences of language. Whatever would have been common among Jesus' Jewish disciples, differences marked by
dominant language would have introduced potential distinctions too at the level of religious structures: myth, ritual, the
divine, and systems of purity.[36] Even if we cannot determine
from Acts with specificity or certainty the nature of those
differences, that there were such differences is entailed by the
language choices that Luke has made.

On the basis of these five considerations, then, I have
sought to counter the view that the presenting problem in
Acts 6:1 is merely "practical" in nature. I have urged, instead, that Luke has provided not-so-subtle direction for us
to understand that the "neglect" depicted here is a symptom
with a far more profound etiology, that in fact the problem is
deeply theological. It has to do with the nature of the gospel
itself and with the embodiment of the gospel in the church.

If, from the perspective of Luke's narrative, the problem
introduced in 6:1 must be understood in theological terms,
it can hardly be the case that the solution would be something other than theological. Thus, the commonly held view
that the apostles hit upon delegation as a key ingredient of
effective leadership[37] is problematic because of its failure to
work theologically with what Luke has given us. Actually, it
is problematic in two other ways as well. First, it assumes
without warrant that Luke presents the apostles as authorized representatives of the narrator's perspective (and, thus,
of the divine perspective, which the narrator represents and
mediates in Luke-Acts). Accordingly, when the apostles deny
the appropriateness of abandoning the word of God in favor

---

36. For this pattern of religious structures, see William E. Paden, *Religious
Worlds: The Comparative Study of Religion* (Boston: Beacon, 1994).

37. Among recent commentators this view is supported by, for example, Mikeal
Parsons, *Acts*, Paideia (Grand Rapids: Baker Academic, 2008), 83–84.

of waiting on tables, their words are taken as a reasonable assessment of things. On the one hand, we might be tempted to imagine that, as authorized representatives of Jesus (see, e.g., Luke 22:28–30), the apostles represent God's agenda accurately. On the other hand, we should not overlook the fact that "authorization," or "legitimation," cuts both ways. Legitimacy justifies the position of a person or group, but at the same time it sets boundaries around that person or group's behavior; their status is legitimate insofar as they operate within the boundaries of their legitimation.[38] Rather than representing the nature of the gospel, the apostles, I am arguing, have transgressed the good news.[39]

Indeed, rather than presuming that the apostles are above reproach, we ought to wonder about the opposite. Was it not under their watch that the disciples had digressed from their idyllic state of unity and violated the character of their own community as one in which "there was not a needy person among them" (4:34)?

Second, the solution that the apostles propose ought to strike a sharp note of discord in our hearing. Can one serve the word and not care for widows? Can one serve the word and not serve at table? These may appear to be practical issues, but for Luke they are theological through and through. This is not only due to the status allocated to widows in the narrative of Luke-Acts, as we have noted earlier; it is also because Luke has already developed the language of διακονία (diakonia, "service") in terms that belie the possibility that these phrases might refer to segregated responsibilities. Is not Jesus himself one who serves at table (Luke 22:24–27; cf. 12:37), with διακονέω (diakoneō, "serve") understood not in its sense of attending to someone at a meal but instead

---

38. See Charlotte Seymour-Smith, *Macmillan Dictionary of Anthropology* (London: Macmillan, 1986), 166.

39. That the Jerusalem apostles are in need of ongoing conversion is transparent later in the narrative of Acts, in 11:1–18, where their criticism of Peter for sharing in the hospitality of gentiles is overturned by Peter's explanation.

metaphorically with regard to providing leadership in carrying out a mission that puts into practice the good news of God? That is, even if, in some theoretical world, we might allow for differentiation of kinds of "service," this is not the case in the world of the Acts narrative. The apostolic task is simply *diakonia* (1:17, 25), and the same is true of Paul's commission (20:45; 21:19).[40]

In other words, the apostles' failure is measured first by the neglect of Hellenist widows and then by their attempt to fracture into distinct parts the singular ministry (*diakonia*) modeled for them by Jesus. This failure is not simply the practical one that would allow relief of the poor to be carried out in a more efficient way. Rather, it surfaces in their allowing a wedge to be driven between the Hellenists and Hebrews such that the most vulnerable of their community—doubly marginal, first as Hellenists among an Aramaic-speaking majority and then as widows among the minority group—suffer need at the basic level of daily sustenance. This is not "good news to the poor" (Luke 4:18 CEB).

This line of interpretation is furthered by the choice of the seven to engage in *diakonia*. First, given their Greek (and Latin) names, their movement into positions of service signifies the decentralizing of the Aramaic-speaking apostles and, then, an affirmation of the Greek-speaking Jewish followers of Jesus. Second, as is widely recognized, their *diakonia* within Luke's narrative is manifestly not waiting on tables; it is the *diakonia* of preaching and evangelism. Rather than dismissing Luke's narration as incoherent, it makes more sense to assume coherence by allowing the actual nature of their *diakonia* to clarify the nature of the *diakonia* suffering neglect in 6:1–7. This would be putting into play a gospel

40. For διακονία in Luke, see the helpful perspective in Turid Karlsen Seim, *The Double Message: Patterns of Gender in Luke and Acts* (Nashville: Abingdon, 1994), 81–87 (though Seim reads Acts 6:1–7 differently [see pp. 108–12]). On the term more generally, see John N. Collins, *Diakonia: Re-interpreting the Ancient Sources* (New York: Oxford University Press, 1990).

that did not allow differences between Hellenist and Hebrew followers of Jesus to resolve themselves into disunity and conflict at the table.[41] Accordingly, it is no surprise that, from among the seven, Stephen goes on to provide the theological bridge that moves the mission outside Jerusalem, and Philip is the first missionary Luke names who takes the gospel to Samaria and, indeed, to the end of the earth.[42] The new missionary leadership, drawn from among the Hellenists, receives its authorization from this: they are witnesses, as Jesus had directed, "in Jerusalem, in all Judea and Samaria, and to the end of the earth" (1:8, my translation).

Having cleared the ground, so to speak, it now remains to ask how best to make sense of Luke's aim in this narrative account. The inclusio marked by the repetition of πληθύνω (*plēthynō*, "increase") in 6:1, 7 makes clear the interest of this narrative account in "growth" and allows us to follow its progression in three steps: from growth to impediment to growth, and from impediment to growth to (renewed) growth. Here is a simple illustration of the analysis by Aristotle (*Poetics* 1450b) of a "narrative" as possessing a beginning, middle, and end—a perspective on narrative that includes but transcends the passing of time in order to claim some sort of meaningful, even necessary, set of relationships among the events that, in narrative, order time.

From the foregoing discussion, we can now see the nature of the problem and its resolution. This scene in Acts 6:1–7 is

41. That this is so was signaled already in the Pentecost event, narrated in Acts 2:1–13, in which the outpouring of the Spirit does not diminish but rather enlivens "difference," marked by language. Ecclesial unity is not dependent on linguistic conformity. See Joel B. Green, "'In Our Own Languages': Pentecost, Babel, and the Shaping of Christian Community in Acts 2:1–13," in *The Word Leaps the Gap: Essays on Scripture and Theology in Honor of Richard B. Hays*, ed. J. Ross Wagner, C. Kavin Rowe, and A. Katherine Grieb (Grand Rapids: Eerdmans, 2008), 198–213.

42. Although for Acts, "end of the earth" probably refers more generally to "gentiles" (see 13:47, with its citation of Isa. 49:6; see further Isa. 8:9; 45:22; 48:20; 62:10–11), Strabo (*Geography* 1.1.6) repeats the view of Homer that Ethiopians live at "the end of the earth."

an indictment against the apostles for their failure to practice the *diakonia* modeled for them by Jesus (Luke 22:24–27), their failure to be the Spirit-generated community of the baptized (Acts 2:42–47), their failure to embody the message of the resurrection of the Lord Jesus (Acts 4:32–35). The result of this theological failure is a fracture in the community, setting Hellenist against Hebrew, which surfaces in the neglect of the widows who now qualify as needy persons among them. By way of resolution, Luke portrays the authorization of fresh leadership for the mission, with this leadership drawn from among the minority of the Jerusalem community. The narrative turns its focus on two of their number, and the apostles as "the twelve" disappear into the shadows, returning to center stage only sparingly in subsequent chapters.[43] This is not to say that, in terms of "what actually happened," the apostles lost their prominence; rather, it is to say that Luke's narration of historical events characterizes people and narrates the cycle of events in relation to the missionary mandate that Jesus had set forth in 1:8: "to the end of the earth."

## Conclusion

This, then, is the theologically potent narrative representation of historical events that Luke has given us. It is not an unbiased presentation. It is not a scientific account of what really happened. This is not because of Luke's failure as a historian but rather because all history writing is partial—incomplete and perspectival.

Of course, someone might want to write a new history of early Christianity. I hope, however, that anyone who might choose to undertake that task will recognize the nature of the

43. Actually, 6:2 contains the only reference to "the twelve" (οἱ δώδεκα) in Acts. References to "the apostles" congregate especially in relation to the Jerusalem council and apostolic decree, though, as a group, they have no particular voice there (15:2, 4, 6, 22, 23; 16:4). In the narrative subsequent to our textual unit (6:1–7), see otherwise 8:1, 14, 18; 9:27; 11:1.

undertaking. Reading Acts as a "narrative representation of historical events" is simply a different enterprise than reading Acts from the standpoint of Historical Criticism₁ and the related assumptions of the Historical-Critical Paradigm. Historical Criticism₁ might view Acts as a source for its work of querying what actually happened in the early years of the Christian movement. Reading Acts in this way is not "scientific," however, but is the first step in the production of another partial narrative. And it is yet another illustration of the inherently antitextual agenda of Historical Criticism₁ and Historical Criticism₂. One can follow the rubrics of Historical Criticism₁ as a historian of early Christianity, or one can read the narrative of Acts theologically, but one cannot do both at the same time. One can follow the instincts of those committed to the Historical-Critical Paradigm, but the end result of such an inquiry will not be a theological reading of the Acts of the Apostles; it will be the substitution of one's own historical narrative for the one that the church has received and regards as Christian Scripture.

# 3

## Scripture and Classical Christology

*The "Rule of Faith" and Theological Interpretation*

I have urged that, whatever else it does, theological interpretation emphasizes the potentially mutual influence of Scripture and doctrine in theological discourse and, then, the role of Scripture in the self-understanding of the church and in critical reflection on the church's practices. This way of describing the work of theological interpretation necessarily raises the question "What is the status of Christian doctrine in and for theological interpretation of the Bible?"

By "doctrine," I refer to the "communally authoritative teachings regarded as essential to the identity of the Christian community";[1] this stands in contrast to "theology," which I take to refer to ongoing critical reflection on the practices of

1. Alister E. McGrath, *The Genesis of Doctrine: A Study in the Foundation of Doctrinal Criticism* (Grand Rapids: Eerdmans, 1990), 11–12.

the church in view of its theological norms.[2] Doctrine, then, is a relatively stable, narrative-shaped set of affirmations that together comprise the parameters of the Christian church as a community of discourse and serve hermeneutically as the pattern by which the church interprets and evaluates its life. For purposes of this chapter, by "doctrine" I refer especially to the emerging Rule of Faith and its codification in the ecumenical creeds of the early church. I recognize that particular theological and ecclesial traditions point to additional creedal statements for what they take to be true and constitutive of their identity, but I leave these to the side in the present discussion because I do not regard them as constitutive of the identity of the church universal. Accordingly, I might phrase my opening question in these terms: "What is the status of the Rule of Faith in and for theological interpretation of the Bible?"

## Scripture and the Rule of Faith

Two observations will suggest the importance of this question. First, from a historical perspective, we cannot argue that the church's Rule of Faith is built on top of the foundation provided by the Old and New Testaments. To put things more pointedly, we cannot argue that the church has simply received its doctrine from the Bible. This observation is based on the recognition that, whatever else may be said of the process that led to the formation and recognition of the two-Testament canon of Christian Scripture, this process had not been completed in the first or second centuries of the Christian movement. That is, the canon of Christian Scripture was not in place at the very time that the Rule of Faith—or Rule of Truth, as it was sometimes called—was taking shape among early church theologians. The New Testament as a canonical

2. Charles M. Wood observes, "Christian theology is a critical inquiry into the truthfulness of Christian witness" (*The Formation of Christian Understanding: An Essay in Theological Hermeneutics* [Philadelphia: Westminster, 1981]), 28.

collection took shape alongside and in relationship to these kerygmatic formulations, so that the least we can say is that, historically, the Rule of Faith and the canon of Scripture took shape in a context of mutual influence. Indeed, one of the primary criteria by which these books, and not those, would compose the New Testament was their coherence with the kerygma as this was articulated in the Rule of Faith.

Second, we know that Israel's Scriptures can be read from a variety of perspectives and, indeed, were read from a variety of perspectives at the time of Jesus and the emerging Jesus movement. One of the characteristics of those early followers of Christ was that they read the Scriptures in a certain way, working with a hermeneutics that located the advent, life, ministry, death, and resurrection of Jesus as the focal point of God's aims in creation and exodus. Pharisees had their own ways of reading these same Scriptures, as did the Qumran sectarians, and so on. What separated those religious communities that turned to the Scriptures that we now call the Old Testament were not differences in their views of scriptural authority or radically different exegetical techniques. Their distinctives cannot be explained by claiming that one group had a stronger grasp of the Hebrew language than the other, or that one had a more compelling assessment of the historical veracity of the events narrated in Israel's Scriptures. Rather, they had different hermeneutical assumptions about how to render the Scriptures faithfully within their own communities. Hence, they turned to the same words but heard them differently. Each community took advantage of the range of possible readings offered by these texts in order to pursue an interpretive agenda that contributed to their own community's identity and formation—and, indeed, legitimacy. Hence, what makes a "Christian reading" of Israel's Scriptures (rather than, say, a Pharisaic or Essene reading of those same Scriptures) are especially those theological lenses by which the followers of Christ have identified the God of Abraham, Isaac, and Jacob with the God who raised Jesus from the dead; and those christological lenses by which those same followers of

Christ have understood that Israel's Scriptures speak of Christ and then the restoration of God's people in the work of Christ such that the church, composed of Jew and gentile, finds its own history within the pages of these Scriptures. These hermeneutical lenses came to be codified in the Rule of Faith.

These two observations illustrate historical and theological warrants for the claim that theological interpretation of Scripture cannot escape the question of the relationship between those ecumenical creeds that define the faith of the church and this canonical collection that we embrace as Scripture. Nevertheless, I recognize that this claim is controversial on more than one ground.

For example, in making this claim, I have called into question, however implicitly, interpretive principles that affirm the perspicuity of Scripture—the view that the message of Scripture is clear and readily available to the average reader. In recent decades this view has been developed in a particular direction, with some assuming that reading the Bible correctly—and today "correctly" is usually parsed in terms of grammatico-historical exegesis—will necessarily lead to an orthodox interpretation of Scripture. Some assume that the biblical materials themselves compel readings that align themselves with the classical faith of the church. I reject this view. My position is that, taken on their own terms and without recourse to a history or community of interpretation, these texts are capable of multiple interpretations, many of which could be understood as "good readings" (i.e., readings supported by careful analysis of the text),[3] but not all of which are worthy of the name "Christian." Thus, even if we want to affirm that scriptural engagement is inescapable for the Christian community, *sola Scriptura* can never guaran-

---

3. It almost goes without saying that, following Umberto Eco (e.g., *The Limits of Interpretation*, Advances in Semiotics [Bloomington: Indiana University Press, 1990]), I maintain that texts are capable of a plurality, though not an infinite number, of interpretations, and thus I opt out of the pursuit of that holy grail of historical-critical scholarship: the one correct meaning. See further Joel B. Green, *Seized by Truth: Reading the Bible as Scripture* (Nashville: Abingdon, 2007).

tee that one is Christian. Most of us have our own anecdotal evidence for how a plain reading of a biblical passage has been used to support sheer nonsense; the Internet is bristling with additional, viable exemplars of my point. This recommends the practice of theological formation as a prerequisite or corequisite for practicing the craft of biblical interpretation. It also proposes at least two contenders for the title "The Great Problem Facing the Church": is the church's great problem *biblical illiteracy*, or is it *theological amnesia*? (I say both.)

At the same time, any attempt to correlate biblical canon and ecumenical creed will excite dissent among modern biblical scholars, who will worry that the church's doctrines will be read back into the Bible. How can one take seriously the church's theology and at the same time allow the Bible to speak on its own terms, according to its own intentions? They will worry that biblical texts will be reduced to the role of a marionette attached to doctrinal strings, a puppet whose speech is that of fourth-century ventriloquists. The degree to which such worries are well founded will depend, of course, on how the relationship between Scripture and Rule of Faith is conceived.

Confronted with the question of the relationship between biblical text and Christian creed, many will assume that the problem should be understood in terms of source and continuity: can these biblical documents support the theological weight placed on them by later creedal formulations? For example, can we find in the texts of the Bible an adequate foundation for the later, explicit, confessional claims of Jesus' divinity? Does the Bible teach that our God is a triune God? As I have already begun to suggest, to my way of thinking, the issue lies elsewhere, in what we might call "the battle for the Bible." I refer not to the battle over the nature of the Bible's authority[4] but rather to questions about what constitutes a faithful reading of the Scriptures. The problem is a hermeneutical one.

4. This was the focus of the book by this title: Harold Lindsell, *The Battle for the Bible* (Grand Rapids: Zondervan, 1976).

Consider, for example, a second-century "battle for the Bible." Irenaeus noted how gnostics made use of biblical exegesis in their arguments, but he insisted that they did not read the Scriptures aright on account of their disregard of the "order and connection" of Scripture. Failing to understand the Bible's true content, they put the pieces of the biblical puzzle together in a way that contravenes the message of Scripture.

> Such, then, is their system, which neither the prophets announced, nor the Lord taught, nor the apostles delivered, but of which they boast that beyond all others they have a perfect knowledge. They gather their views from other sources than the Scriptures; and, to use a common proverb, they strive to weave ropes of sand, while they endeavour to adapt with an air of probability their own peculiar assertions the parables of the Lord, the sayings of the prophets, and the words of the apostles, in order that their scheme may not seem altogether without support. In doing so, however, they disregard the order and the connection of the Scriptures, and so far as in them lies, dismember and destroy the truth. By transferring passages, and dressing them up anew, and making one thing out of another, they succeed in deluding many through their wicked art in adapting the oracles of the Lord to their opinions. Their manner of acting is just as if one, when a beautiful image of a king has been constructed by some skilful artist out of precious jewels, should then take this likeness of the man all to pieces, should re-arrange the gems, and so fit them together as to make them into the form of a dog or a fox. (*Against Heresies* 1.8.1)[5]

The "order and connection" to which Irenaeus referred was the Rule of Faith, a summary of the Christian kerygma that measured faithful interpretation of Scripture. Writing of this stage in the church's history, William Abraham observes:

> The development of a scriptural canon was utterly inadequate to meet the challenge posed by the Gnostics. The Gnostics

5. *ANF* 1:326.

had no difficulty accepting any canon of Scripture which might be proposed; being astute in their own way and eclectic in their intellectual sensibilities, they simply found ways to use Scripture to express their own theological convictions. This should come as no surprise to anyone. A list of diverse books merely by the sheer volume involved is susceptible to a great variety of readings.[6]

In short, the church has long recognized the need for a "ruled reading" of its canonical texts, and this again presses the question of how Scripture functions vis-à-vis the creed.

In fact, the relationship between the Rule of Faith and our readings of Scripture can be construed in various ways. I have already begun to sketch my understanding of the relationship between Scripture and creed, but let me make this clear with reference to five ways to conceive of that connection.

(1) We do not use the Rule of Faith to predetermine the meaning of the Bible or to read later doctrinal formulations back into the Bible.

(2) Nor do we imagine that the Rule of Faith is the superstructure that has the Scriptures as its substructure.

Actually, these two approaches could be assumed by persons on either side of the debate—for example, by those who insist that the Bible teaches a trinitarian theology and by those who deny that this is so. However, these construals of the relationship between canon and creed are problematic on historical grounds, as we have already seen. Depending on how these approaches are formulated, they may be suspect on hermeneutical grounds as well. This is because they seem generally to assume a "container" approach to "meaning," as if the interpretive enterprise were merely occupied with finding what was already resident in the text, as if "meaning" were nothing other than a property of the text. Supporting such an interpretive approach, Claude Lévi-Strauss spoke of a work of art

6. William J. Abraham, *Canon and Criterion in Christian Theology: From the Fathers to Feminism* (Oxford: Oxford University Press, 1998), 36.

as "an object endowed with precise properties, that must be analytically isolated, and this work can be entirely defined on the grounds of such properties"; accordingly, one should approach a work of art, like a literary text, "as an object which, once created, had the stiffness—so to speak—of a crystal; we [confine] ourselves to bringing into evidence these properties."[7] In reply, Umberto Eco observed, "A text is not a 'crystal.' If it were a crystal, the cooperation of the reader would be part of its molecular structure."[8]

(3) Again, we should not imagine that the ecumenical creeds simply summarize the "stuff" of the Bible. One interpreter put it to me in these terms: imagine the Bible as a tube of toothpaste; the Rule of Faith is what comes out when we squeeze the tube.

Friedrich Schleiermacher, widely regarded as "the father of Protestant theology," illustrates well the problem of this third possibility in a statement that appears at the head of his discussion of "The Formation of the Dogmatic System":

> All propositions which claim a place in an epitome of Evangelical [i.e., Protestant] doctrine must approve themselves both by appeal to Evangelical confessional documents, or in default of these, to the New Testament Scriptures, and by exhibition of their homogeneity with other propositions already recognized.[9]

Schleiermacher thus underscores helpfully, and programmatically, such crucial concerns as the significance for Christian theology of classical formulations of the faith; the import of addressing Scripture theologically, and from an avowedly theological stance (and, by implication, the decisive role of the theological formation of readers of Scripture); and the place of coherence in theology. Problematically, however, Schleiermacher's use of "New Testament" to modify "Scriptures"

---

7. Cited in Umberto Eco, *The Role of the Reader: Explorations in the Semiotics of Texts*, Advances in Semiotics (Bloomington: Indiana University Press, 1979), 3–4.
8. Ibid., 37.
9. Friedrich Schleiermacher, *The Christian Faith* (Philadelphia: Fortress, 1928), 127.

makes explicit what has been and, in some circles, continues to be the practice associated with theology in its negative regard for or dismissive stance toward the status and role of the Old Testament as Christian Scripture. More generally, Schleiermacher's choice underscores how easily any attempt to summarize the "stuff" of the Christian Bible gives way to a summary of some part of the Bible. This is true even if those who attempt to summarize the "stuff" of the Christian Bible are typically not as explicit about their canon within the canon. In view of my present discussion, though, especially troublesome is Schleiermacher's clause "in default of these," which suggests that the church's confessional documents so fully summarize the biblical witness that we need to resort to the Scriptures only when an issue is raised on which the creed is silent. In its potential and actual dislocation of Scripture, this would be the antithesis of theological interpretation of Scripture.

In my view, the relationship between Scripture and doctrine can be helpfully conceptualized in two ways, both of which are intrinsically hermeneutical.

(4) In early patristic exegesis the notion of "economy" was paramount because, it was held, correct interpretation of Scripture must express its overall order or structure. As John J. O'Keefe and R. R. Reno summarize, for Irenaeus and others, "the true and accurate reading of scripture . . . must follow the divine economy by which God has put together the mosaic of scripture."[10] According to Richard Burnett's important analysis of Karl Barth's theological exegesis, Barth similarly urged that the "whole" within which the parts of the Bible must be comprehended was its unified witness to God.[11] From this vantage point, our choices are not reduced to those usually presented us—for example, that we allow the

---

10. John J. O'Keefe and R. R. Reno, *Sanctified Vision: An Introduction to Early Christian Interpretation of the Bible* (Baltimore: Johns Hopkins University Press, 2005), 37.

11. Richard E. Burnett, *Karl Barth's Theological Exegesis: The Hermeneutical Principles of the* Römerbrief *Period* (Grand Rapids: Eerdmans, 2004), 77–78.

creeds to overrun the biblical text or hold the creeds at bay so as not to spoil our close readings of the biblical texts. Already in the first century, creedal traditions (e.g., from the simple acclamation "Jesus is Lord" [1 Cor. 12:1] to more developed formulas such as 1 Cor. 15:3–5 represents) served to unify the Christian movement and to clarify its faith in the context of its challengers, and the later, ecumenical creeds would likewise speak to the integrity of the Christian church and its faith. Taking with utter seriousness, then, the diversity of voices and perspectives within Scripture and among the biblical books, we find unity in the Rule of Faith, that "divine economy by which God has put together the mosaic of scripture."[12] Procedurally, then, a theological hermeneutic might be well advised to ask, "What do we see as we read Scripture through the prism of the creeds that we would not otherwise see?"

(5) Finally, a theological interpretation of Scripture can inquire whether our readings of the Old and New Testaments lie within the parameters set by the Rule of Faith. Accordingly, the Bible might be read from all sorts of positions, and we might argue that biblical texts can mean all sorts of things. But we say that readings of the Old and New Testaments that do not cohere with the Rule of Faith are not Christian readings of the Scriptures. This fifth possibility is the one that presently interests me, since I am concerned with what happens when an otherwise apparently faithful reading of Scripture stands in tension with a claim of the ecumenical creeds of the church.

---

12. It is important to recognize this strategy for what it is. Perhaps the biggest challenge for proponents of "biblical theology" is the unity and diversity in the Bible. One of the typical solutions practiced among contributors to "New Testament theology" is to examine the theologies of each New Testament document before inquiring into the possibility of an underlying synthesis. The consequent unity can hardly escape its being conceptualized as thematic propositions and its status as one interpreter's understanding of the lowest common denominator among the variety of witnesses. This fourth proposal is quite different, since it assumes that unity is not found inside the biblical texts but underneath them, in God's economy as this is understood in the narrative terms of the Rule of Faith.

## The Bible, the Creed, and Body-Soul Dualism

What happens when an otherwise apparently faithful reading of Scripture stands in tension with a claim of the ecumenical creeds of the church? This is not an abstract question for me. I have championed a reading of Scripture that, at least on the surface of things, seems to contradict some early, ecumenical formulations of the Rule of Faith. I refer to the theological anthropology of the Bible. In my book *Body, Soul, and Human Life: The Nature of Humanity in the Bible*[13] I have argued that, according to the Scriptures, we do not *possess* souls but simply *are* souls. That is, I have supported from Scripture and in conversation with the neurosciences the position that, as human persons, we are characterized by the indivisibility of our embodied human lives. We have no need for recourse to a second entity, such as soul or spirit, in order to explain human capacities and distinctives. This view of the human person is generally called "monist," over against a dualistic view. As some concerned critics have reminded me, however, this reading of the Scriptures stands in tension with assertions in both the Athanasian Creed and the Chalcedonian Definition of the Faith that Jesus is composed "of a rational soul and human flesh."

Note that my critics have not queried my conclusions on exegetical grounds. They have not sought to undermine my actual readings of biblical texts on historical, philological, or grammatical grounds. The question that they have pressed bears repeating: what happens when an otherwise apparently faithful reading of Scripture stands in tension with a claim of the ecumenical creeds of the church? Several responses are possible. For example, my guess is that most Christians today have never heard of either the Athanasian Creed or the Chalcedonian Definition of the Faith. Why draw attention to phrases found among the classical creeds only in these two? Since the more well-known Apostles' Creed and Nicene

---

13. Joel B. Green, *Body, Soul, and Human Life: The Nature of Humanity in the Bible*, STI (Grand Rapids: Baker Academic, 2008).

81

Creed seem not to be worried about bodies and souls, why should we?

Alternatively, if we were to imagine that the Bible provided the foundation on which the creeds gained their content and authority, we might simply remark that, on this point, we take the Bible over the creeds. When the Bible and the Rule of Faith disagree, so much the worse for the Rule of Faith!

I have argued for a more organic relationship between Scripture and creed, however, so I need to take a different path. I will first remark briefly on the scriptural case for monism, then turn to discuss the issue as it is raised in the Athanasian Creed and the Chalcedonian Definition of the Faith.

Neither the Old nor the New Testament evidences a sustained argument regarding the "essence" of the human being, though everywhere we find evidence that the human person ought to be characterized in relational terms. A case favoring a monist view of the human person in Scripture would account for considerations such as the following four.

(1) Although the theological tradition has often identified the creation of humanity in the divine image with the human possession of a soul, this view cannot be supported in Scripture. How to understand the divine image is the object of a long-standing debate, though Scripture itself supports views that accord privilege to human capacities or vocation, and not to human essences or parts.[14] Moreover, according to Genesis 2:7, a human being does not *possess* a soul but rather *is* a soul (in Hebrew, *nepeš*)—or, to translate the Hebrew phrase in a way that makes more sense, Adam "became a living being." The CEB is even more helpful: "The Lord God formed the human from the topsoil of the fertile land and blew life's breath into

---

14. The literature is voluminous; among recent contributions, see J. Richard Middleton, *The Liberating Image: The* Imago Dei *in Genesis 1* (Grand Rapids: Brazos, 2005); W. Sibley Towner, "Clones of God: Genesis 1:26–28 and the Image of God in the Hebrew Bible," *Int* 59 (2005): 341–56; Stanley J. Grenz, *The Social God and the Relational Self: A Trinitarian Theology of the Imago Dei*, Matrix of Christian Theology (Louisville: Westminster John Knox, 2001).

his nostrils. The human came to life." Moreover, according to Genesis 1:30, it is not only humans who are "soulish" in this sense, but so too are the beasts of the earth, the birds of the air, and everything that creeps on the earth, since, like human beings, they are characterized by *nepeš*; that is, all God's creatures, human and otherwise, share the breath of life.

(2) Neither the Old Testament nor the New Testament employs a specialized vocabulary from which someone might claim that certain words require an affirmation of body-soul dualism. Hence, it will not do simply to find the word "body" or the word "soul" in a biblical text and assume on this basis that Scripture has asserted a particular view of the essence or essences (or parts) composing a human. The Greek term sometimes translated as "soul," ψυχή (*psychē*), does not, on its own, refer to the soul of body-soul dualism. Interestingly, Aristotle could write an entire book titled *Concerning the Soul* without holding to the position of body-soul dualism, whether Platonic or otherwise.

(3) Nor do we have a basis any longer for imagining that differences in cultural background mean that even though the Old Testament assumes or bears witness to anthropological monism, the New Testament supports a dualist rendering of the human person, body and soul. The idea that the Greco-Roman world of Peter and Paul was dualist in its anthropology belies the complexity of philosophical views that inhabited the world in which the New Testament writings appeared and overlooks the widespread influence of Stoicism, itself a monist philosophy, in the New Testament world. There was a range of views among philosophers and medical writers of this period, and with few exceptions Jewish views continued to affirm the oneness of the human person witnessed in Israel's Scriptures. What is more, we cannot escape the degree to which the New Testament writers followed the path of anthropological monism set out by the Old Testament in their theological understanding of the human person.

(4) Finally, the Old and New Testaments treat issues of human healing and health, and salvation itself, in surprisingly holistic terms. Accordingly, it makes little sense to think of Jesus addressing someone's spiritual needs versus bodily needs. Instead, Jesus addressed (embodied) human needs, period.

Of course, persons committed to a form of body-soul dualism will hardly be convinced by this brief sketch and might argue that numerous philosophical issues and exegetical points require further conversation. I would agree. But my concern here is neither to support fully a monist anthropology nor to convince dualists of the error of their ways. I do not expect to have so easily convinced anyone otherwise. My own view is that once we have been taught, whether by Plato or Descartes or someone else, to think of the human person in terms of body-soul dualism, with the "self" typically identified with the soul, it seems only natural that many would open the pages of the Christian Scriptures to find body-soul dualism. This may seem especially true in the modern West, where "souls" are so much the stuff of prime-time television and summer reading, but it is also true that other people have their own traditions and experiences that lend support to a dualist anthropology.[15]

15. Consider, for example, the ubiquity of "near-death" experiences and other types of "out-of-body" experiences, which seem to have led people long ago to think of themselves as a soul or spirit inhabiting a body. This is because such experiences represent in phenomenological terms a kind of disembodied version of what we would eventually come to know as Cartesian dualism. Carol Zaleski regards the widespread nature of near-death experiences as evidence of the immortality of the soul, which she regards as the basis of Christian hope in the afterlife (*The Life of the World to Come: Near-Death Experience and Christian Hope* [New York: Oxford University Press, 1996]). This argument flies in the face of the stubbornness with which the Christian tradition has held tightly to the creedal affirmation of "the resurrection of the body" (see Caroline Walker Bynum, *The Resurrection of the Body in Western Christianity, 200–1336*, Lectures on the History of Religions n.s. 15 [New York: Columbia University Press, 1995]). Reports of out-of-body experiences are well known from ancient times to the present in folklore, mythology, and religious narratives (for bibliography, see Olaf Blanke et al., "Linking Out-of-Body Experience and Self Processing to Mental Own-Body Imagery at the Temporoparietal Junction," *Journal of Neuroscience* 25, no. 3 [2005]: 551; idem, "Out-of-Body Experience and Autoscopy of

Within the Christian theological tradition, this tendency is probably no less typical, since theologians over the centuries often have identified the uniqueness of the human person vis-à-vis nonhuman creatures in terms of the human possession of a soul. That this theological position is often articulated in terms of erroneous linguistics (e.g., about what σῶμα [*sōma*] and ψυχή [*psychē*] "mean" in the Bible) or on the basis of erroneous exegesis (especially the identification of the "soul" with the "image of God" in Gen. 1) is generally beside the point. I recognize that I am swimming against the current—that is, the sheer inertia of long-standing claims regarding body-soul dualism. However, it is not my concern here to convince my readers that the witness of Scripture is congruent with a monist anthropology. (For that, I direct them to my aforementioned book *Body, Soul, and Human Life*.)[16] Instead, my concern is to address the criticism that in taking this position I have interpreted the Bible in a way that apparently stands in tension with certain formulations of the Rule of Faith.

Stated succinctly, my reply is to deny that these creedal statements affirm body-soul dualism. Instead, they affirm Jesus' full humanity, an affirmation that my reading of the Scriptures in no way transgresses. To put it differently, the creedal statements in question are focused on christological arguments and are not concerned with theological anthropology per se. In affirming Jesus' full humanity, however, these creedal statements employ nonbiblical categories and an erroneous science, with the result that they use the problematic language of "rational soul and human flesh" in order to secure their affirmation of Jesus' full humanity. We can begin to follow what has happened by investigating the use of the phrase "rational soul."

---

Neurological Origin," *Brain* 127 [2004]: 244). For discussion of these phenomena and rejection of their status as evidence for body-soul dualism, see Joel B. Green, "What about . . . ? Three Exegetical Forays into the Body-Soul Discussion," *CTR* n.s. 7 (2010): 3–18.

16. See also Green, "What about . . . ?"

## The "Rational Soul" of the Creeds

The Chalcedonian Definition of the Faith begins,

> We, then, following the holy Fathers, all with one consent, teach people to confess one and the same Son, our Lord Jesus Christ, the same perfect in Godhead and also perfect in humanity; truly God and truly human, of a rational soul and body [ἐκ ψυχῆς λογικῆς καὶ σώματος, *ek psychēs logikēs kai sōmatos*], coessential with the Father according to the Godhead, and consubstantial with us according to the humanity.[17]

Similarly, the Athanasian Creed affirms that the Lord Jesus Christ "is God and human," developing this affirmation, in part, by the phrase "Perfect God: and perfect human, of a reasonable soul and human flesh subsisting [*ex anima rationali et humana carne subsistens*]."[18] This claim is later repeated: "For as the reasonable soul and flesh is one person [*nam sicut rationalis et caro unus est homo*]: so God and human is one Christ."[19] The question that I want to pursue involves the significance of the expression "reasonable soul" or "rational soul."

The phrase λογικὴ ψυχή (*logikē psychē*), "rational soul," is used at the turn of the era as a shorthand for referring to an aspect of the soul expounded in Plato. By the end of the fourth century AD, however, what once was a terminological gloss had become thoroughly standardized and Neoplatonized.

Neither Plato nor Aristotle uses the phrase in any of his surviving works, but it was used later among writers discussing Platonic and Aristotelian ideas and attributed to Greek philosophers in a handful of fragments. Plato had spoken of a complex inner person, however, a soul composed of either

---

17. From Philip Schaff, *The Creeds of Christendom: With a History and Critical Notes*, rev. Davis S. Schaff, 6th ed., 3 vols. (Grand Rapids: Baker, 1983 [1931]), 2:62. In representing this translation, I have retained Schaff's own emendations. Here and below, I also have edited translations of ancient texts for inclusive language with regard to human beings.

18. Ibid., 2:69.

19. Ibid.

two or three species or powers,[20] the most important in either version being reason or rationality (λόγος [*logos*, "reason"] or λογιστικός [*logistikos*, "endued with reason, rational"]). In many cases in ancient sources, "soul" simply denotes a human person. This usage is found in, for example, Acts 27:37, where Luke writes, "In all, there were two hundred and seventy-six of us [αἱ πᾶσαι ψυχαί, *hai pasai psychai*] on the ship" (CEB). But "soul" could also be used of nonhuman creatures. Modifying a "soul" as "rational" would immediately signal that the author was talking about humans rather than plants or animals.

The earliest reliable instances of the phrase "rational soul" come from the first-century Alexandrian Jew Philo, who worked with Platonic categories by distinguishing between irrational souls (created with the bodies of humans and animals) and rational souls (created earlier, prior to their taking up lodging in human bodies). Following Stoic and medical theories of the soul,[21] he identified the irrational soul with the blood, and the superior or rational soul with the mind. Sketching the creation of the world by God, Philo observes in *On the Creation of the World* 66 that, as the crowning glory of creation, "He made man, and bestowed on him mind *par excellence*,"[22] which he then labels "the soul of the soul" (ψυχῆς τινα ψυχήν, *psychēs tina psychēn*) (my translation).[23]

20. His favored terms were γενεά (*genea*, "class, kind") and εἶδος (*eidos*, "class, kind") rather than, say, μέρος (*meros*), which would signify "part." It is difficult to imagine "parts" of something that were regarded as immaterial. See Paul S. MacDonald, *History of the Concept of Mind: Speculation about Soul, Mind and Spirit from Homer to Hume* (Aldershot, UK: Ashgate, 2003), 37–54; T. M. Robinson, "The Defining Features of Mind-Body Dualism in the Writings of Plato," in *Psyche and Soma: Physicians and Metaphysicians on the Mind-Body Problem from Antiquity to Enlightenment*, ed. John P. Wright and Paul Potter (Oxford: Oxford University Press, 2000), 37–55.

21. See Heinrich von Staden, "Body, Soul, and Nerves: Epicurus, Herophilus, Erasistratus, the Stoics, and Galen," in Wright and Potter, eds., *Psyche and Soma*, 79–116.

22. English translation in Philo, *Philo*, 10 vols., trans. F. H. Colson and G. H. Whitaker, LCL (Cambridge, MA: Harvard University Press, 1929–62), 1:51.

23. See Eduard Schweizer et al., "ψυχή κτλ.," *TDNT* 9:635.

More interesting for our purposes, though, is Philo's special-ized use of the phrase in *On Planting* 18–19, where he equates the "rational soul" with the image of God in Genesis 1:

> Accordingly, the great Moses has not compared the nature of the rational soul [τῆς λογικῆς ψυχῆς, *tēs logikēs psychēs*] to anything created, but spoke of it as the image of that di-vine and invisible Spirit—as though it were a coin stamped and impressed by God's seal, the engraving of which is the everlasting Word. For he says, "God breathed into his face the breath of life." (my translation)

Philo identifies the soul with God's image similarly in *On the Creation of the World* 69:

> After all the rest, as I have said, Moses tells us that human-ity was created after the image of God and after his likeness [Gen. 1:26]. Right well does he say this, for [nothing] earth-born is more like God than humanity. Let no one represent the likeness [of God] as one to a bodily form; for neither is God in human form, nor is the human body God-like. No, it is in respect of the mind, the sovereign element of the soul, that the word "image" is used.[24]

As I have earlier hinted, for Philo, Genesis provides two ac-counts of the creation of humanity. Again attributing the authorship of Genesis to Moses, he writes in *On the Creation of the World* 134–135,

> After this he says that "God formed man by taking clay from the earth, and breathed into his face the breath of life" [Gen. 2:7]. By this also he shows very clearly that there is a vast difference between the man thus formed and the man that came into existence earlier after the image of God [i.e., ac-cording to Gen. 1:26–28]: for the man so formed is an object of sense-perception, partaking already of such or such quality,

24. Philo, *Philo*, 1:55.

consisting of body and soul, man or woman, by nature moral; while he that was after the (Divine) image was an idea or type or seal, an object of thought (only), incorporeal, neither male nor female, by nature incorruptible.

It says, however, that the formation of the individual man, the object of sense, is a composite one made up of earthly substance and of Divine breath: for it says that the body was made through the Artificer taking clay and moulding out of it a human form, but that the soul was [made originated] from nothing created whatever, but from the Father and Ruler of all: for that which He breathed in was nothing else than a Divine breath.[25]

Going on at length to prove the splendor of the human body that God created, Philo remarks how God chose the very best clay, the most pure material to form the body; after all, "a sacred dwelling-place or shrine was being fashioned for the reasonable soul [ψυχῆς λογικῆς, *psychēs logikēs*], which man was to carry as a holy image, of all images the most Godlike" (*On the Creation of the World* 137).[26] Here and elsewhere in his writings, then, we find a Platonizing interpretation of the relevant passages in Genesis 1–2, whereby Genesis 1:26–27 concerns the creation of the invisible, immortal human being, and Genesis 2:7 recounts the creation of the visible, mortal human.

More significant for our purposes is usage among the church fathers of the second and third centuries. Thus, in Clement of Alexandria we have the beginning of what will become a standard Christian usage. For example, in *Stromata* 5.14 he says,

Rightly then Moses says, that the body which Plato calls "the earthly tabernacle" was formed of the ground, but that the rational soul was breathed by God into man's face. For there, they say, the ruling faculty is situated; interpreting the access by the senses into the first man as the addition of the soul. (*ANF* 2:466)

25. Philo, *Philo*, 1:107.
26. Philo, *Philo*, 1:109.

Note here how for Clement, as for Philo, Platonic categories provide the hermeneutical lens for reading the Genesis accounts. Thus, "Wherefore also humanity is said 'to have been made in [God's] image and likeness.' For the image of God is the divine and royal Word, the impassible human; and the image of the image is the human mind" (*Stromata* 5.14 [*ANF* 2:466]). Throughout Clement's work the "rational soul" is the governing seat of the human being, the location of the intellect, and even that which is addressed by God. The language and thought of Clement, Tertullian, and Origen are reminiscent of what we find in Philo, but each would adopt Middle Platonism and possibly even Neoplatonism, for which the rational soul would be the most characteristic human self.[27]

So thoroughly has Platonic thought made its mark that Tertullian titles the sixteenth chapter of his treatise *On the Soul* "The Soul's Parts: Elements of the Rational Soul." He begins, "That position of Plato's is also quite in keeping with the faith, in which he divides the soul into two parts—the rational and the irrational."[28] Tertullian goes on to emphasize the importance of the rational element, how it is the seat of communion with God and Christian living, in contrast with the irrational element, which is under the control of sin and the devil.[29]

It is in Origen's work that we find the most extensive use of the phrase "rational soul." Origen appears to agree wholly with Clement and Tertullian on what the rational soul is, but he develops his thought further. He says, for example, in *Against Celsus* 4.18:

> But if one were to take the change as referring to the soul of Jesus after it had entered the body, we would inquire in what sense the term "change" is used. For if it be meant to

---

27. See the discussion of Plotinus, founder of Neoplatonism, in Richard Sorabji, *Self: Ancient and Modern Insights about Individuality, Life, and Death* (Chicago: University of Chicago Press, 2006), 118–26.

28. *ANF*, 3:194.

29. See the helpful analysis in M. C. Steenberg, *Of God and Man: Theology as Anthropology from Irenaeus to Athanasius* (London: T&T Clark, 2009), 55–103.

apply to its essence, such a supposition is inadmissible, not only in relation to the soul of Jesus, but also to the rational soul of any other being.[30]

Notice that Origen simply assumes that a soul could "enter the body" and that no rational soul could ever undergo an essential change. In *Against Celsus* 8.51 he seems to agree with Celsus's Platonic anthropology:

> In the next place, [Celsus] expresses his approval of those who "hope that eternal life shall be enjoyed with God by the soul or mind, or, as it is variously called, the spiritual nature, the reasonable soul, intelligent, holy, and blessed"; and he allows the soundness of the doctrine, "that those who had a good life shall be happy, and the unrighteous shall suffer eternal punishments."[31]

This is especially telling because Origen finds a point on which he and Celsus agree: the nature of the "reasonable soul," collocated now with "soul," "mind," and "spiritual nature." In classical Platonism the "rational soul" is really a shorthand way to refer to a particular species or power of the trifunctional soul. For Origen, it simply *is* the soul. That is, the notion of soul has narrowed from what it once was. Especially interesting for our purposes is the hallmark of the rational soul: its identification with the "image of God." For example, elsewhere in *Against Celsus* Origen claims that human beings "have been created in the image of God, for the image of the Supreme God is his reason" (4.85).[32]

The story continues into the fourth century, of course, but the main lines are already clear. My point thus far is simply this: a phrase never found in Scripture, "rational soul," has a lengthy prehistory in the classical period; bypassing any reflection among New Testament writers, this phrase underwent

30. *ANF* 4:504.
31. *ANF* 4:658.
32. *ANF* 4:535.

philosophical and then theological development to the point that, in the thought of some church fathers, it came to refer to a constitutive part of the human person.

Of course, after the New Testament era the church bore witness to some variety with regard to its understanding of the soul. Nevertheless, Kallistos Ware's review of "the soul in Greek Christianity" identifies two pervasive views: first, body and soul typically were regarded as two complementary entities composing an undivided unity; and second, an identification of the "image of God" with the soul was based on a reading of Genesis 1:26–27 (and 2:7).[33] Indeed, many, though not all, link the divine image with the soul while excluding the body from participation in God's image. Interestingly, Ware also calls attention to the degree to which these writers have drawn on Platonic ideas rather than on Scripture. That is, following a path blazed by Philo, the generally monist views of Scripture have been displaced through the ascendency of generally dualist views among early church theologians.

One more step is needed in order to move from theological anthropology to the christological claim that Jesus is composed "of a rational soul and human flesh" in the Athanasian Creed and Chalcedonian Definition. At issue in these confessional statements was how best to portray the nature of the incarnation. Read within the regnant, dualist theological anthropology of the postapostolic church, an affirmation that Jesus was composed "of a rational soul and human flesh" is at least a way of saying that *Jesus is a human being*. However, read in relation to christological debates of the time, it is much more. It is a way of saying, further, that *Jesus is fully a human being*. This was necessary because of the point of view, soon to be relegated to the category of heresy, that the incarnation consisted in this: a human body in which the divine Logos dwelled.

---

33. Kallistos Ware, "The Soul in Greek Christianity," in *From Soul to Self*, ed. M. James C. Crabbe (London: Routledge, 1999), 50–51. Ware refers only to Genesis 1:26–27, but the importance of Genesis 2:7 is underscored in Steenberg, *Of God and Man*.

In a debate that traded on the pervasive view that the human being was made up of two "substances" (even if much about those two substances was debated, including the origin of the soul and how the two, body and soul, were connected), Apollinaris had denied that Christ had a "rational soul" or "human mind" or "human spirit," arguing instead that the divine Logos took over the functions of the human soul or mind. Others maintained in response that the rational soul was essential to human personhood, and that Christ must have assumed a rational soul if the whole of the human being was to be restored. The rational soul of a person requires salvation too.[34] Against Apollinarian Christology, Gregory of Nazianzus wrote in *Letters* 101.7:

> Anyone who has placed his hope in a human being who lacked a human mind is himself truly mindless and does not deserve a complete salvation. For "what was not assumed was not healed." . . . If it was half of Adam that fell, then half might be assumed and saved. But if it was the whole of Adam that fell, it is united to the whole of him who was begotten and gains complete salvation.[35]

As Theodore of Mopsuestia later would write in *On the Nicene Creed* 5.9–11:

> The disciples of Arius and Eunomius say that he took a body but not a soul; the divine nature, they say, supplied the place of a soul. They abased the divine nature of the Only-Begotten to such an extent that, declining from its natural grandeur, it performed the actions of the soul, imprisoning itself in that body and performing the functions necessary for the body's existence.

34. On this complex of issues, both in terms of the ancient debate and of contemporary christological discussion, see F. LeRon Shults, *Christology and Science* (Grand Rapids: Eerdmans, 2008), 21–62.

35. Cited in John Anthony McGuckin, ed., *We Believe in One Lord Jesus Christ*, Ancient Christian Doctrine 2 (Downers Grove, IL: IVP Academic, 2009), 148.

Theodore counters:

> It was necessary that the Son should assume not only a body but also an immortal and rational soul. It was not only the death of the body that he had to abolish, but also the death of the soul, which is sin.[36]

This was necessary if Jesus was to be fully human and if the incarnation was to have its most comprehensive soteriological significance.

Observe how the logic works here. The basic claim is this: Jesus is fully human. That this is the basic claim is inescapable from the parallels in the Chalcedonian Definition, where "humanity" is juxtaposed with "truly human," which is juxtaposed with the phrase "like us in all things," which stands in parallel with the phrase "of a rational soul and body." To articulate their affirmation of Jesus' full humanity, the church fathers turned to the categories of ancient Greek science and philosophy—not the categories of Scripture, but those of the ancient and developing Platonic tradition. Working from within these categories, the church fathers parsed the claim that Jesus is fully human in terms of body-soul dualism, and this claim made its way into these creedal affirmations in these terms: "of a rational soul and human flesh."

All this depends on a philosophical-scientific view of humanity understood as the combination of two substances, body and (rational) soul. Not even the writers of the New Testament came under the influence of this stream of the Platonic tradition, however, with the result that we look in vain for references to a "rational soul" in the New Testament. We also look in vain there for patterns of the soul found in these later writers, who attribute the will to sin to the soul, who attribute immorality to the soul, or who have it that the body, a thing corporeal, must be governed by a thing incorporeal, a soul. Nevertheless, the humanity of Jesus is never in doubt

36. Cited in ibid., 149–50.

in the Scriptures; indeed, 1 John actually makes explicit what a false prophet might erroneously deny: the embodied life of Jesus Christ (4:1–3).

I conclude, then, that my understanding of the witness of the Scriptures to theological anthropology may stand in tension with a particular anthropology assumed by the christological claim made by the Athanasian Creed and the Chalcedonian Definition of the Faith, but in no way does my interpretation of the monist anthropology of the Scriptures stand in tension with the kerygmatic affirmation of Jesus' true humanity essential to these two creedal statements.

## The Mutual Relationship of Scripture and Creed

The example that I have sketched can be pushed further to suggest the importance of careful reflection on the relationship between Scripture and creed. It will not do, I have suggested, simply to make Scripture the foundation on which to build the creed, or to make the creed in some sense the foundation for rendering the meaning of Scripture. My sense is that the best way to characterize their relationship is in terms of dialectic or, perhaps better, mutual influence. Thus, we can appropriately ask, as I have, whether our readings of Scripture are congruent with the Rule of Faith.

Following a different path, we might also ask this question: were we to engage the Christian Scriptures from the perspective of the Rule of Faith, what might we see that otherwise we are blinded to seeing? Were we to adopt this hermeneutical perspective, for example, we might find reason to promote trinitarian readings of the opening of 1 Peter or the Markan account of the baptism of Jesus, readings that would be eclipsed by other concerns were we to read from perspectives uninformed by the Rule of Faith—for example, from the perspective of historical criticism.

Locating canon and creed in relation to each other in these ways, we might also wonder about points at which the narrative of the Rule of Faith seems to be lacking. We might wonder, for example, about the ease with which the Apostles' Creed passes over the significance of Jesus' life in the short space between the two affirmations "born of the virgin Mary, suffered under Pontius Pilate." That the New Testament devotes four of its books to narrations of Jesus' ministry registers a level of importance for the story of Jesus that seems overlooked by the Apostles' Creed. Moreover, the repeated appeals to "the faithfulness of Jesus" in the New Testament letters presume some significance for the story of the life of Jesus of Nazareth. Again, however, this importance seems not to be embraced by the Apostles' Creed —a lacuna that has repercussions both for Christology (and especially for our understanding of Jesus' sonship)[37] and for discipleship (i.e., for those who "follow the example of Jesus").[38] Other questions might be raised as well, not the least of which is the general lack of interest in the creeds regarding Israel and the exodus, or the creeds' underdeveloped eschatology.

On the one hand, we might imagine that this lacuna is not as significant as it might seem, since, as I have already urged, the role of the Rule of Faith is not best articulated in terms of its providing a fulsome "summary" of Scripture. If the creed is not so much a synopsis or précis of Scripture as it is a "rule" for reading Scripture, then why be overly concerned about such gaps? On the other hand, lacking a well-articulated emphasis on the character of Jesus' life and mission, we might neglect to fill out more fully what it means to affirm, with John 14 or Hebrews 1, that Jesus is the definitive revelation of God. Without this emphasis,

37. See Richard N. Longenecker, "The Foundational Conviction of New Testament Christology: The Obedience/Faithfulness/Sonship of Christ," in *Jesus of Nazareth, Lord and Christ: Essays on the Historical Jesus and New Testament Christology*, ed. Joel B. Green and Max Turner (Grand Rapids: Eerdmans, 1994), 473–88.

38. See William C. Spohn, *Go and Do Likewise: Jesus and Ethics* (New York: Continuum, 2000).

we might erroneously imagine that orthodoxy (right belief) can easily be untethered from orthokardia (right heart) and orthopraxis (right action). We might overlook the unambiguous significance of Israel in the plotline of God's story. We might miscalculate the comprehensive significance of the biblical witness to the end as the restoration of all things. And so on.

This series of "What if?" questions does not really undermine the importance of the creeds for biblical interpretation, however. Instead, they underscore my claim that the ecumenical creeds of the church ought not simply trump the work of biblical interpretation but instead must be placed in a dialectical relationship with Scripture that is mutually informative.

## Conclusion

The discerning reader may grasp the lack of direct correspondence between my argument for the importance of the creeds in theological interpretation and my work on the theological anthropology assumed by the christological claims of the Athanasian Creed and the Chalcedonian Definition of the Faith. This is because I have urged that, in this instance, we are not dealing with a bona fide point of tension between Scripture (with its apparent monist anthropology) and creed (with its presumed dualist anthropology). This is because the creeds are not "about" the nature of the human person as such. Instead, I have urged that, on the affirmation of Jesus' true humanity central to these creeds, Scripture and creed speak with one voice, even though they do so in different vernacular. That is, although I have called into question the portrait of the human person assumed by these creedal statements, I have in no way undermined their Christology. Again, here Scripture and creed do not stand in tension. Nevertheless, I have admitted that the creed is limited in its understanding of the human person such that if we were to engage in doctrinal criticism, we might ask how we might better formulate the Christology affirmed in Scripture and creed.[39]

For theological interpretation generally, the more critical question remains of how to work at the interface of canon and creed. For theological interpretation, I take this problematic as a given, since there is no ecclesially grounded interpretation of Scripture that can first ignore or dispose of the doctrine that sets the parameters of ecclesial identity and, by extension, by which the church determines what is a Christian reading of its Scriptures. The question, then, is how the ancient creeds of the ecumenical church might serve their hermeneutical role. I have argued in favor of two possibilities. First, procedurally, a theological hermeneutic might ask, "What do we see as we read Scripture through the prism of the creeds that we would not otherwise see?" If Scripture is always read within a context, then we can inquire what it means to read Scripture in relation to the creed. Second, I have urged that theological interpretation of Scripture can inquire whether our readings of the Old and New Testaments lie within the parameters set by the Rule of Faith. This second approach takes seriously that the diverse body of texts to which we turn as Christian Scripture is capable of being read in ways that make sense of the grammar and historical particularity of these texts but lie outside the parameters of Christian faith. Coherence with the Rule of Faith, then, would serve as one, but not the only, criterion of a Christian reading of the Bible.

---

39. See Shults, *Christology and Science*.

# 4

# John Wesley, Wesleyans, and Theological Interpretation

*Learning from a Premodern Interpreter*

For some, contemporary interest in theological interpretation may seem to be no more than a throwback to the days of "precritical" exegesis. This characterization is not altogether without basis, since theological interpreters tend almost universally to speak of the importance of premodern scriptural interpretation,[1] significant attempts are well under way to make more accessible the exegetical work of our forebears,[2] and some have gone so far as to champion

1. See, for example, Stephen E. Fowl, introduction to *The Theological Interpretation of Scripture: Classic and Contemporary Readings*, ed. Stephen E. Fowl, Blackwell Readings in Modern Theology (Cambridge, MA: Blackwell, 1997), xvii–xviii.

2. See especially the following series: The Ancient Christian Commentary on Scripture, edited by Thomas C. Oden (Downers Grove, IL: InterVarsity); The Church's Bible, edited by Robert Louis Wilken (Grand Rapids: Eerdmans); Blackwell Bible Commentaries, edited by David Gunn et al. (Oxford: Wiley-Blackwell).

the superiority of precritical exegesis[3] or even to pattern their own interpretive work on it.[4]

Why should those interested in theological interpretation of Scripture look backward as they mark the way forward? Two reasons come immediately to mind. First, the conventions and protocols of historical approaches have exercised such influence and become so pervasive in the West (and, increasingly, in biblical studies globally) that we find ourselves bereft of good models for practicing theological interpretation. One way forward, then, is to look backward at the character of biblical interpretation prior to the modern period and the hegemony of historical-critical interests.[5] Second, one of the hallmarks (and handicaps) of modernity is its sense of unease regarding tradition and, more generally, the past. In fact, in an earlier essay I urged that impetus for the contemporary segregation of biblical studies and theology could be traced in part to the problematizing of "history" associated with modernity[6]—to what Carl E. Schorske names as that characteristically modernist impulse to define itself "not so much *out* of the past, indeed scarcely *against* the past, but detached from it."[7] It follows, then, that late modernity or postmodernity would find itself exploring in fresh ways the traditions out of which it has been sculpted.

Renewed openness to traditional forms of biblical interpretation raises important questions for persons interested

3. David C. Steinmetz, "The Superiority of Pre-critical Exegesis," *ThTo* 37, no. 1 (1980): 27–38.

4. For example, Telford Work, *Deuteronomy*, BTCB (Grand Rapids: Brazos, 2009); see the critical remarks in Seth Heringer, "The Practice of Theological Commentary," *JTI* 4 (2010): 133–36.

5. Of course, given the vitality of theological interpretation within Orthodox Christian circles, this is not the only possibility. See, for example, Timothy Clark, "Recent Eastern Orthodox Interpretation of the New Testament," *CBR* 5 (2007): 322–40.

6. Joel B. Green, "Modernity, History, and the Theological Interpretation of the Bible," *SJT* 54 (2001): 308–29.

7. Carl E. Schorske, *Thinking with History: Explorations in the Passage to Modernism* (Princeton, NJ: Princeton University Press, 1998), 3–4.

today in theological interpretation, not the least of which is the degree to which one locates oneself ecclesially. This, after all, was until recently one of the defining features of engagement with the biblical materials. Indeed, here we are close to the heart of what it means to involve oneself in theological interpretation of Christian Scripture. The question is not simply whether one reads the Bible in the service of the church, but whether this "service," these ecclesial commitments, actually determine the protocols by which one reads the Bible as Scripture. We may put the question sharply: should it make a difference in how one reads the biblical materials whether one is reading self-consciously from within a state-supported university department of religious studies in the United States or from within the church? Champions of the Historical-Critical Paradigm, which I sketched at the beginning of chapter 2, would be required by that paradigm to answer in the negative. Biblical studies is simply biblical studies, regardless of the location of the student of the Bible. Practitioners of theological interpretation reply in the affirmative.

Of course, this raises—indeed, has raised[8]—the question of whether theological interpretation is worthy of the label "scholarship." This is because scholarship has failed to make a crucial distinction between "objectivity" and "neutrality." Following Thomas Haskell's helpful perspective on the matter,[9] I take "objectivity" to refer to those commitments and practices that are definitive of scholarly discourse, such as openness to a perspective outside of one's own, commitment to fairness and honesty in interpretation, and the capacity for self-reflexivity—commitments and practices that make possible thoughtful community. Haskell refers to objectivity as

8. See my programmatic comments in the introduction to this book.
9. Thomas L. Haskell, "Objectivity Is Not Neutrality: Rhetoric versus Practice in Peter Novick's *That Noble Dream*," in *Objectivity Is Not Neutrality: Explanatory Schemes in History* (Baltimore: Johns Hopkins University Press, 1998), 145–73.

a kind of "detachment": "that frail and limited but perfectly real power that, for example, permits conscientious scholars to referee one another's work fairly, to acknowledge merit even in the writings of one's own critics, and successfully to bend over backwards when grading students so as not to penalize those holding antagonistic political convictions."[10] Persons working from within a theological tradition, whether it be Pentecostal or Wesleyan or Orthodox or Reformed, can engage in scholarship understood according to these terms. "Neutrality," however, refers to "selflessness," to "truth seeking as a matter of emptying oneself of passions and preconception, so as to become a perfectly passive and receptive mirror of external reality."[11] "Neutrality," often mistaken for "objectivity," is not only an impossibility for the theological interpreter but also an unrealistic, undesirable, and, indeed, impossible aspiration for any sort of exegete.

It has become commonplace in many circles to grant the impossibility of what I have defined as "neutrality" in biblical interpretation, but admissions of this sort have yet to lead to a wholesale reimagining of the task of biblical studies. From the perspective of theological interpretation, the character of Scripture itself presses the issue. For example, to what degree can a text that articulates the importance of care for aliens, orphans, and widows be effectively engaged by persons who adopt a neutral or disengaged position with regard to society's marginal?

In any case, the central question becomes whether we are able and willing to recognize our commitments, since failure to do so does not keep us from having those commitments but rather increases the probability that we will unwittingly regard our commitments as simply the way things are for all people in all places and, more to the point in the present context, as simply "the plain meaning of Scripture."

10. Ibid., 149.
11. Ibid., 150.

I began to address the issue of the ecclesial location of theological interpretation in chapter 3, centering there on the interrelationship between biblical studies and the (ecumenical) rule of faith. Now pushing this question further, I think it worth inquiring into how one's own ecclesial and theological tradition—in my case, the Wesleyan-Methodist tradition—might shape a theological hermeneutic. In what follows, I will not so much attempt to sketch a contemporary Wesleyan theological hermeneutic as to identify some landmark features of such a hermeneutic.[12] I will undertake this agenda by illustrating and reflecting on a particular specimen of Wesley's own theological interpretation. After some comments on Wesley's approach to reading Scripture, I will turn to his treatment of 1 Peter 1:1–2.

## John Wesley: A Precritical Exegete?[13]

Reacting against medieval modes of interpretation, Protestant Reformers tended toward an emphasis on the one meaning of Scripture and produced hermeneutical handbooks with criteria for legitimate readings—especially philological, including the historical exigencies governing the meaning of words. At the turn of the nineteenth century, new emphases on historical context led interpreters to stress the distance between text and reader, and to construe this distance primarily

12. For more programmatic remarks, see Joel B. Green, "Reading the Bible as Wesleyans," *WTJ* 33 (1998): 116–29. For a range of possible Wesleyan interpretive strategies, see Barry Callen and Richard P. Thompson, eds., *Reading the Bible in Wesleyan Ways: Some Constructive Proposals* (Kansas City, MO: Beacon Hill, 2004). Regarding theological interpretation, though, see especially the important work of Steven J. Koskie, "Reading the Way to Heaven: A Wesleyan Theological Hermeneutic of Scripture" (PhD diss., London School of Theology–Brunel University, 2010).

13. What follows is adapted from Joel B. Green, "Theological Interpretation and John Wesley," in *The Continuing Relevance of Wesleyan Theology: Essays in Honor of Laurence Wood*, ed. Nathan Crawford (Eugene, OR: Pickwick, 2011), 222–33 (used by permission of Wipf & Stock Publishers).

in historical terms. Consequently, biblical study began to devote its energies first to mapping this distance and then, in some cases, to discussions about how to traverse this distance. For many, recognition of the historical chasm separating the known world of our contemporaries from the strange world of the Bible had its impetus in a concern to protect the biblical materials from easy conscription into the service of modern concerns, including the church's theology. These emphases have cultivated various forms of "higher criticism" characteristic of the Historical-Critical Paradigm, which has until recently defined the scholarly engagement with the Bible.

What of the hermeneutics of John Wesley? When Wesley is read against the backdrop of these developments, it is no surprise that we find him branded with that most marginalizing of modern epitaphs: uncritical.[14] Such indictments typically bemoan the fact that Wesley gave little notice to the sacred cows of the Historical-Critical Paradigm, especially the original meaning of a biblical text according to the (reconstructed) historical context and/or the (reconstructed) intent of the author. Accordingly, we might imagine that anyone attempting to take Wesley seriously as a biblical interpreter would similarly be charged either with pursuing an agenda of naive primitivism, interested in recovering precritical modes of interpretation, or with attempting to escape wholesale the alleged perils of higher criticism of the Bible.

Let me offer five grounds for denying that an attempt to learn theological interpretation from Wesley is an escape into precritical exegesis. The first and most obvious is the simple absurdity of assuming that the only style of reading worthy of the designation "critical" is modern historical criticism.

14. See, for example, Wilbur H. Mullen, "John Wesley's Method of Biblical Interpretation," *Religion in Life* 47 (1978): 99–108 (esp. 106–7); Duncan S. Ferguson, "John Wesley on Scripture: The Hermeneutics of Pietism," *Methodist History* 22 (1984): 234–45 (esp. 238, 244); George A. Turner, "John Wesley as an Interpreter of Scripture," in *Inspiration and Interpretation*, ed. John F. Walvoord (Grand Rapids: Eerdmans, 1957), 156–78 (esp. 165–66).

The critical tradition is far more inclusive, with a variety of disciplined approaches available to adjudicate among alternative renderings of biblical texts.[15]

Second, to say that we might learn from Wesley is not the same thing as saying that we must recover, index, and repeat Wesley, as though Wesley's modes of theological exegesis might function as the unchanging laws of the Medes and Persians. We and Wesley live on opposite ends of the modern era of historical criticism, and we cannot act as though we have nothing to learn from the intervening years. Nor, however, should we imagine that the intervening years have obliterated the significance of Wesley's work with Scripture. Persons in the Wesleyan tradition might consider how best to participate in a discerning *ressourcement*, even if it means that we might struggle with one another in identifying those points at which Wesley needs to be corrected or broadened.

Third, classifying Wesley as "precritical" overlooks the degree to which Wesley himself took seriously the currents of learning in his own day. In his reading of the Gospel of Matthew, for example, questions about science and theology surfaced on account of Jesus' miracles. In Matthew 4:23–25 the evangelist summarized the nature of Jesus' ministry throughout Galilee as proclamation and healing, and this combination is continued throughout the Gospel. Thus, immediately following the Sermon on the Mount (Matt. 5–7), Matthew reports a series of miracles concerned with healing (Matt. 8–9) as he depicts Jesus as one who makes available the presence and power of God's kingdom to those dwelling on the margins of society in Galilee—a leper, the slave of a gentile army officer, an elderly woman, the demon-possessed, a paralytic, a collector of tolls, a young girl, and the blind. With the seventeenth-century emergence of the "new science," what challenges would face interpreters of such texts as these?

15. See M. H. Abrams, *The Mirror and the Lamp: Romantic Theory and the Critical Tradition* (New York: Oxford University Press, 1953); Hazard Adams, ed., *Critical Theory since Plato*, rev. ed. (Fort Worth: Harcourt Brace Jovanovich, 1992).

Wesley lived in an age of exciting, unprecedented scientific discovery, when mysteries of all sorts had begun to be explained in terms of natural causes, as one might expect of a world influenced by Newtonian mechanics. He was aware that some educated people had begun to question Jesus' miracles. Consequently, in his note on Jesus' commission to the disciples that they should "cast out devils" (Matt. 10:8), Wesley observed that someone had said that diseases ascribed to the devil in the Gospels "have the very same symptoms with the natural diseases of lunacy, epilepsy, or convulsions," leading to the conclusion "that the devil had no hand in them." Wesley continues,

> But it were well to stop and consider a little. Suppose God should allow an evil spirit to usurp the same power over a man's body as the man himself has naturally, and suppose him actually to exercise that power; could we conclude the devil had no hand therein, because his body was bent in the very same manner wherein the man himself bent it naturally?
>
> And suppose God gives an evil spirit a greater power to affect immediately the origin of the nerves in the brain, by irritating them to produce violent motions, or so relaxing them that they can produce little or no motion, still the symptoms will be those of over-tense nerves, as in madness, epilepsies, convulsions, or of relaxed nerves, as in paralytic cases. But could we conclude thence, that the devil had no hand in them?[16]

Reading Wesley's comments, we might forget that serious study of the central nervous system and its relationship to human behavior was barely a century old. Nevertheless, elsewhere Wesley says, "For six or seven and twenty years, I had made anatomy and physic the diversion of my leisure hours."[17]

16. John Wesley, *Explanatory Notes upon the New Testament* (London: Epworth, 1975 [1754]), 53. In my citations of Wesley I have introduced inclusive language in reference to humans.

17. John Wesley, "A Plain Account of the People Called Methodists," XII.2 (in John Wesley, *The Works of John Wesley*, 14 vols., 3rd ed., ed. Thomas Jackson [Grand Rapids: Baker, 1979 (1872)], 8:264).

In this way, he documented for us his interest in the new vistas that science had begun to open and his intent to take seriously the importance of science for biblical interpretation and for Christian mission. At this juncture his solution appears to be openness to the truth of both faith and science; rather than deny the truth either of stories of demonized persons in the Gospels or of scientific explanations, he allows that both could be true.

Fourth, we see emerging in Wesley's *Explanatory Notes upon the New Testament* the beginnings of an interest in the sort of historical background about which modern biblical studies is most serious.[18] I say "beginnings" because, in his own description of how he engages with biblical texts, we see a decidedly unmodern approach to dealing with difficult texts. "Does anything appear dark or intricate?" he asks. For most students of the Bible formally trained in our colleges, universities, and seminaries, the key to making sense of difficult passages in the Bible is to seek more background, more historical detail, more insight into ancient patterns of thought and behavior. Wesley's approach takes a different route.

> Does anything appear dark or intricate? I lift up my heart to the Father of lights: "Lord, is it not your Word, 'If any lack wisdom, let them ask of God'? You 'give generously and ungrudgingly.' You have said, 'If any be willing to do your will, they shall know.' I am willing to do, let me know, your will." I then search after and consider parallel passages of Scripture, "comparing spiritual things with spiritual." I meditate thereon, with all the attention and earnestness of which my mind is capable. If any doubt still remains, I consult those who are experienced in the things of God, and then the writings whereby, being dead, they yet speak. And what I thus learn, that I teach.[19]

18. For a similar judgment, see Robin Scroggs, "John Wesley as Biblical Scholar," *JBR* 28 (1960): 418.

19. John Wesley, "Preface," *Sermons on Several Occasions* 5 (in Wesley, *Works*, 5:3).

That is, faced with a biblical text that is unclear, Wesley (1) looks to God for help, (2) compares the text with other biblical passages, (3) meditates, (4) consults with "those who are experienced in the things of God," and (5) looks to commentaries and other published works for assistance.[20] (Note how Wesley presents some of these interpretive procedures in phraseology borrowed from the Bible itself.) This is not to suggest that, for Wesley, historical detail was unimportant. In a stinging reversal of much contemporary biblical interpretation, though, Wesley operates with the assumption that the primary chasm that must be overcome if we are to make sense of Scripture is mapped not in terms of our need for more historical detail but with reference to our need to know God and to embrace God's ways. "I lift up my heart to the Father of lights. . . . I am willing to do, let me know, your will." Here is a clear window into the kind of knowledge, the kind of truth that Wesley sought in Scripture.

On the one hand, then, his *Explanatory Notes upon the New Testament* and many of his sermons are dotted with historical data. On the other hand, reading Scripture could never be divorced from the Bible's status as divine word. In the end, Wesley's approach to Scripture can be characterized neither as emphasizing prayer over research nor as prioritizing research over prayer. He held these together, while obviously prioritizing the significance of Scripture for Christian faith and life over the importance of establishing, say, the first-century meaning of a text in its historical context.

Fifth, in what may be a surprising twist, a careful examination of Wesley's biblical interpretation demonstrates the degree to which Wesley worked with, not against, the significance of biblical materials understood within their own settings. I say that this may be surprising because Wesley himself does not make this plain, at least not in such a way that much of contemporary biblical scholarship might

20. See Mullen, "John Wesley's Method," 102.

recognize. This is not only because Wesley does little to pull back the curtains on his exegetical work so as to reveal the inner workings of his interpretive practices; it is also because we do not find in Wesley an explicit interest in the herme- neutical move from "what it meant" to "what it means," nor, indeed, do we find this movement in his hermeneutical practices. Wesley's sermons on the Corinthian correspon- dence, for example, do not first establish what Paul must have meant in the first century so that Wesley could then add a section to his sermon titled "How 1 Corinthians Applies to Us" or "The Relevance of 1 Corinthians for Today." But neither did he imagine that 1 Corinthians had been written in the eighteenth century, as though Paul had set out to ad- dress the theological arguments and everyday concerns of the Methodist movement. Wesley seems to have come to the text aware both of his theological questions and com- mitments and of the origins of the Corinthian letters within the ongoing relationship between the apostle Paul and the Corinthian Christians. Thus, Wesley comes to the text with the working assumption that, as Scripture, 1 Corinthians was written not only for a first-century audience but also for eighteenth-century Christians.

In the remainder of this chapter I want to turn more fully to this fifth point in order to illustrate Wesley's theological interpretation of Scripture. Focusing on 1 Peter, I will show that Wesley's theological concerns are quite different from those of Peter, but also that Wesley's aims are closely aligned with Peter's own central emphases.

## Wesley, 1 Peter, and Predestination

The opening of 1 Peter is important for the way it identifies the character of Peter's model audience. It is also interesting for the space that it opens for Wesley to discuss one of the more debated theological questions of his day. The text of 1 Peter 1:1–2 reads as follows:

Peter, apostle of Jesus Christ, to the chosen, strangers in the world of the diaspora in Pontus, Galatia, Cappadocia, Asia, and Bithynia, according to the foreknowledge of God the Father, in the sanctification of the Spirit, because of the obedience and sprinkling of the blood of Jesus Christ: May grace and peace be multiplied to you.[21]

### The Audience of 1 Peter

Two observations will give us a sense of the significance of this letter opening for 1 Peter as a whole.

First, Peter's readers are designated as "chosen, strangers in the world"; that is, they are both God's elect and alienated from their own worlds. Their lives are a paradox: honored and chosen by God, but dishonored by people and forced to the margins of social life in their own villages and towns. Peter's letter, then, is addressed to folks who are not at home, who do not belong, whose lives are lived on the margins of acceptable society, whose deepest allegiances and dispositions are not well aligned with what matters most in the world in which they live. Dispersion, exile—these are images of trauma, expulsion from the homeland, violence, life on the move, erosion of identity, movement from the center to the periphery of the comfortable and the valued, loss of social and cultural roots, torn from the nourishment of family and tradition, refugees.[22] The letter of 1 Peter has its own register of phrases by which to portray the setting of Peter's audience: "tested by fire" (1:7), abused (2:23; 3:9), suffering (2:23), reviled (3:16), slandered (3:16), "reproached for the name of Christ" (4:14), and "suffering as a Christian" (4:16).

---

21. Translation from Joel B. Green, *1 Peter*, THNTC (Grand Rapids: Eerdmans, 2007), 14.

22. See Daniel L. Smith-Christopher, *A Biblical Theology of Exile*, OBT (Minneapolis: Fortress, 2002); Jan Felix Gaertner, ed., *Writing Exile: The Discourse of Displacement in Greco-Roman Antiquity and Beyond*, Mnemosyne, Bibliotheca Classica Batava Supplementum 283 (Leiden: Brill, 2007).

We can push harder to distinguish what it means that Peter characterizes his audience as strangers in their own land, as exiles. First, exile refers to an in-between time and an in-between place. Exiles live between memories of home and the freedom that comes with stability on the one hand, and hopes of restoration on the other. Second, exile is a time of identity formation. Living at home and among our own people, we think little of what makes us who we are: our idioms, our typical practices, the foods we eat, our habits of work and play, the taken-for-granted conventions that mark our identity. When we live away from home among others, such questions demand fresh attention. Who are we in relation to them? What is the basis of our constitution as a community? What are our characteristic practices? By what strategies do we keep faith with who we are? Third, exile is a time of temptation and testing. The experience of exile resides in this: the social and religious threat confronting a people challenged with the perennial possibility and threat of assimilation and defection. Accordingly, the question arises of how Christians ought to live in the midst of wider social currents that do not honor Jesus as Lord of the whole of life.

Grasping the oxymoronic nature of the situation faced by Peter's audience is important, since we do not easily correlate rejection within the human family with honorable status before God. Peter writes this letter to address precisely this sort of problem. Drawing on the experience of Israel in the Old Testament, Peter develops the concept of "stranger" in what might be surprising ways. He associates being strangers in the world with God's election and, thus, with scriptural themes such as call and vocation, covenant, and journey. His perspective anticipates the words of the second-century *Epistle to Diognetus*, which develop this idea more fully:

For Christians are no different from other people in terms of their country, language or customs. Nowhere do they inhabit cities of their own, use a strange dialect, or live life out of the ordinary. . . . They live in their respective countries, but only as resident aliens; they participate in all things as citizens, and they endure all things as foreigners. Every foreign territory is a homeland for them, every homeland foreign territory. They marry like everyone else and have children, but they do not expose them once they are born. They share their meals but not their sexual partners. They are found in the flesh but do not live according to the flesh. They live on earth but participate in the life of heaven. They are obedient to the laws that have been made, and by their own lives they supersede the laws. They love everyone and are persecuted by all. They are not understood and they are condemned. They are put to death and made alive. They are impoverished and make many rich. They lack all things and abound in everything. They are dishonored and they are exalted in their dishonors. (5:1–14)[23]

The first observation, then, concerns the plight of Christians: God's chosen ones, scorned by the world at large. Second, Peter uses three parallel phrases to underscore that being rejected by humans does not entail having been rejected by God. His audience may be strangers in the world, treated like aliens who do not really belong here, but they have been chosen

- according to the foreknowledge of God the Father;
- in the sanctification of the Spirit; and
- because of the obedience and sprinkling of the blood of Jesus Christ.

Peter thus documents, first, that life on the margins of the world is not a denial of one's chosen status before God. Second, and more important, he shows that it is precisely because of the work of the Father, Son, and Holy Spirit in the

---

23. English translation in *The Apostolic Fathers*, 2 vols., ed. Bart D. Ehrman (Cambridge, MA: Harvard University Press, 2003), 2:139, 141.

lives of believers that they are being rejected. How could it be otherwise? Did the world not reject Jesus? Should we not anticipate, then, that the world would reject those who have been chosen by God and made holy by God's Spirit?

### Wesley on God's Foreknowledge

I have gone into some detail in order to show how the phrase "according to the foreknowledge of God the Father" functions within 1 Peter. Divine choice and alien status are deeply rooted in God's purpose as this comes to expression in the Scriptures. Accordingly, the dissonance of present life—chosen by God but held in contempt in society—is neither a surprise to God nor an obstruction to his plan.

Removed from the work that this phrase performs in the presentation of Christian life in 1 Peter, though, this reference to God's foreknowledge came to support what Wesley regarded as a problematic, even unbiblical idea of predestination. As a result, in his *Explanatory Notes upon the New Testament* he departs from his more usual routine of providing a word of historical background here, an explanation of an important term there. Instead, he outlines a full-blown theological essay on foreknowledge and predestination.

What is predestination? It is not easy to give a straightforward answer, since there are varieties of views in the Christian tradition. Wesley's definitions derive from Calvin's writings and from formalized confessions of faith penned in the sixteenth and seventeenth centuries:

> "Out of the general corruption," says the French Church, "he [God] draws those whom he has elected; leaving the others in the same corruption, according to his immovable decree." "By the decree of God," says the Assembly of English and Scotch Divines, "some are predestinated unto everlasting life, others foreordained to everlasting death." "God has once for all," says Mr. Calvin, "appointed, by an eternal and unchangeable

decree, to whom he would give salvation, and whom he would devote to destruction." (*Inst.*, cap. 3, sec. 7)[24]

In other words, for Wesley, predestination could be understood thus: "By virtue of an eternal, unchangeable, irresistible decree of God, one part of humankind are infallibly saved, and the rest infallibly damned; it being impossible that any of the former should be damned, or that any of the latter should be saved."[25] This is the view that Wesley encountered—and countered. Predestination was a key theological battleground in Wesley's day, and his engagement in the discussion was motivated in no small part by the influence of Calvinism within the Methodist movement. Thus, in his sermon on Romans 8:32, "Free Grace," Wesley outlined seven arguments against this notion of predestination:

1. Predestination makes preaching unnecessary and thus nullifies one of the ordinances of God.
2. Predestination undermines holiness. After all, "If a sick man knows that he must unavoidably die or unavoidably recover, though he knows not which, it is not reasonable for him to take any medication at all."[26]
3. Predestination obstructs the work of the Holy Spirit to bring assurance to the believer and so leads to despair.
4. Predestination destroys the zeal of believers toward works of mercy, such as feeding the hungry or clothing the naked.
5. Predestination renders needless the whole Christian revelation.
6. Predestination introduces contradictions into the message of the Bible.
7. Predestination is an insult to God because it denies God's justice and mercy and portrays God as having

24. John Wesley, "Predestination Calmly Considered," 9 (in Wesley, *Works*, 10:207).
25. John Wesley, "Free Grace," 9 (in Wesley, *Works*, 10:207).
26. Ibid., 11 (in Wesley, *Works*, 7:376).

done the work of the devil in leading people to the gates of hell.[27]

In the place of this problematic notion of predestination, Wesley substitutes his teaching on free grace. This is that God gives his grace to everyone, even if not everyone chooses to receive and to act on this gift. To everyone the choice is put: to choose life, to repent, to come and taste.

What, then, of Wesley's reading of 1 Peter 1:1–2: "chosen . . . according to the foreknowledge of God the Father"? The context within which Wesley reads this text is the theological controversy in which he is enmeshed in eighteenth-century England. Hence, he concerns himself immediately and at length with anyone who might misunderstand Peter's reference to God's foreknowledge as support for the (erroneous) doctrine of predestination.

Wesley's opening salvo is his denial that God has the kind of foreknowledge that we might attribute to God. With the language of "foreknowledge," Wesley writes, God has adopted human vocabulary that is capable of speaking only partially of God's reality. Peter, then, is simply using language that would be understandable to his readers, rather than describing what is more accurately true of God.

> Strictly speaking, there is no foreknowledge, no more than after-knowledge, with God: but all things are known to him as present from eternity to eternity. This is therefore nothing more than an instance of the divine condescension to our lower capacities.[28]

Clearly, what is at stake here is how we view time, and particularly how we understand God's relation to time.

Wesley held a view that is different from what many have assumed about time, though his view was consistent with

27. In Wesley, *Works*, 7:373–86.
28. Wesley, *Explanatory Notes*, 872.

that of a number of early church fathers and also of an important figure in philosophical and theological discussions about time and eternity, Boethius. Popular views regard time in linear terms, marking the progress of time from the past to the present to the future. For Boethius, eternity both included and transcended time. Since God inhabits eternity, it follows that all of time is present to God at once. It therefore makes no sense to say that God "foreknew" such-and-such an event. We might experience time in terms of the past, present, and future, but this is not God's experience. This is because nothing is earlier or later than eternity, which God inhabits. Wesley himself knew and embraced the work of Boethius, and this is the basis of his claim that it is absurd to use the term "foreknowledge" with reference to God. Wesley goes on to urge that God's knowledge of all things does not cause things to happen.

These two claims are closely related, and it is worth hearing Wesley's words at length. First, let us review Wesley's understanding of time:

> When we speak of God's *foreknowledge* we do not speak according to the nature of things, but after the manner of humans. For if we speak properly there is no such thing as either *foreknowledge* or *after-knowledge* in God. All time, or rather all eternity (for time is only that small fragment of eternity allotted to human beings) being present to him at once, he does not know one thing before another, or one thing after another, but sees all things in one point of view, from everlasting to everlasting. As all time, with everything that exists therein, is present with him at once, so he sees at once whatever was, is, or will be to the end of time.[29]

God's experience of time is not the same as our own. Instead, for Wesley, God is omniscient in that he knows all things past, present, and future, because what happened in the past,

---

29. John Wesley, "On Predestination," 5 (in Wesley, *Works*, 2:226–27).

what is happening in the present, and what will happen in the future—all understood according to the way we mark time—are always present to God. But if God knows all things, does this not mean that God causes all things? Not at all.

> But observe: we must not think they are because he knows them. No; he knows them because they are. Just as I (if one may be allowed to compare the things of humans with the deep things of God) now know the sun shines. Yet the sun does not shine because I know it: but I know it because it shines. My knowledge takes it as true that the sun shines, but does not in any way cause it. In like manner God knows that humanity sins; for he knows all things. Yet we do not sin because he knows it: but he knows it because we sin. And his knowledge takes it as true that we sin, but does not in any way cause it. In a word, God looking on all ages from the creation to the consummation as a moment, and seeing at once whatever is in the hearts of all the people, knows everyone that does or does not believe in every age or nation. Yet what he knows, whether faith or unbelief, is in no way caused by his knowledge. People are as free in believing, or not believing, as if he did not know it at all.[30]

Wesley's view of time is thus key to his understanding of foreknowledge and predestination.

It remains, then, to inquire into the true meaning of predestination, or, more particularly, what it means in the words of 1 Peter that people have been chosen "according to the foreknowledge of God the Father." For Wesley, God's "fore-appointment" consists in this: (1) whoever believes will be saved from the guilt and power of sin; (2) whoever endures until the end will be saved eternally; and (3) whoever receives the gift of faith thereby becomes a child of God and receives the gift of the Holy Spirit, which enables one to live as Christ lived.

The way Wesley lays out the life of faith might be called "synergistic," meaning that the life of faith requires cooperation

---

30. Wesley, "On Predestination," 5 (in Wesley, *Works*, 2:227).

between God and the person of faith. As Wesley himself puts it, predestination involves both God and the human being; at every step along the way "[God's] promise and [human] duty go hand in hand. All is a free gift; and yet such is the gift, that the final result depends on our future obedience."[31]

Having followed Wesley through some of the side streets and back alleys of eighteenth-century theological controversy, we may now seem to be far removed from the opening words of 1 Peter. We might even wonder if Peter himself would be amazed at what has become of what must have seemed so simple a phrase, "chosen . . . according to the foreknowledge of God the Father." Or we might wonder how Peter would respond to Wesley's claim, "God looking on all ages from the creation to the consummation as a moment, and seeing at once whatever is in the hearts of all the people, knows everyone that does or does not believe in every age or nation." In reality, though, what is central to Wesley in this whole discussion is not at all alien to Peter's message. Wesley takes a circuitous route to get there, but this is because of the terrain of the theological skirmishes that he was forced to navigate in eighteenth-century Britain. But the synergism for which Wesley argued is no more important to Wesley than it was to Peter.

We may recall that Peter's audience consists of followers of Christ who live paradoxical lives. They are chosen of God but strangers in the world. As strangers in the world, they bear the brunt of the world's scorn, insults, and shame. How will they respond? This is the central matter. Peter directs them along two paths at once. He affirms in no uncertain terms that they have been chosen by God, made holy by the Holy Spirit, and liberated by the atoning death of Jesus. In the world, they are dishonored, but before God they are honored indeed. On the one hand, then, Peter gives them their identity in relation to the threefold work of God.

31. Wesley, *Explanatory Notes*, 872.

On the other hand, from the beginning of this letter to its conclusion, he calls them to certain behaviors in the world. Note, for example, how in 1 Peter 1:3–21 Peter's affirmation of God's graciousness and his analysis of his audience's status before God opens the way for Peter to articulate the nature of their behavior in the world. His message moves from the indicative to the imperative, from "is" to "ought." Thus, on account of God's mercy, believers must set their hope completely on the coming grace (v. 13); on account of God's holiness, believers must become holy in every aspect of life (vv. 14–16); and, on account of the Father's impartial justice and the liberation effected by Christ's sacrificial death, believers must live in reverent fear (vv. 17–21).

Moving further into the letter (1 Pet. 2:21–23), we read that they must follow the example of Christ:

> For to this you have been called, because Christ also suffered for you, leaving you an example, so that you should follow in his steps. "He committed no sin, and no deceit was found in his mouth." When he was abused, he did not return abuse; when he suffered, he did not threaten; but he entrusted himself to the one who judges justly.

They are to set aside the immorality of their former lives, they are to forgo retaliation for the abuse they suffer, and they are to cultivate such Christian practices as doing good, practicing hospitality, and extending themselves in acts of mutual love and service to one another (e.g., 1:22; 3:8–17; 4:7–11, 15, 19). And if they do, then this is the promise they have: "And after you have suffered for a little while, the God of all grace, who has called you to his eternal glory in Christ, will himself restore, support, strengthen, and establish you" (5:10). Is not Wesley's own conclusion, "All is a free gift; and yet such is the gift, that the final result depends on our future obedience," fully at home here?

119

## Conclusion

We have been able to follow some of the contours of Wesley's theological interpretation of Scripture and to begin to identify some of the landmarks of a contemporary theological hermeneutic for those numbered among his heirs. Unlike more recent participants in the enterprise of theological interpretation, John Wesley's exegetical work is interesting in that he neither tried to make peace with historical criticism while reading Scripture theologically nor engaged in theological interpretation as an alternative to (or as a denial of) historical criticism. This, of course, is a product of his historical moment. Situated as he was on the front end of the historical-critical movement, Wesley's works witness the importance of historical considerations without imagining that historical inquiry might overwhelm the church's need to hear God's voice in Scripture, or that historical inquiry might claim to provide without remainder the "meaning" of a biblical text. Wesley's theological exegesis is interesting in part, then, because he had no need to adopt a defensive stance vis-à-vis historical-critical methods and commitments.

What, then, was the design of his theological interpretation? In the example from 1 Peter that I have sketched, Wesley demonstrates (1) the need for interpretation—that is, the simple reality that the words of Scripture are not self-interpreting—and in this case the way philosophical considerations can bear on how we read a biblical text; (2) the importance of context in interpretation—in his case underscoring the ecclesial and theological contexts within which God's foreknowledge is understood; and (3) the simultaneity of Scripture—that is, the capacity of the biblical text to speak as divine word in the first century as well as the eighteenth. More needs to be said about Wesley's practices of theological interpretation, especially as this is witnessed in his *Explanatory Notes upon the New Testament* and sermons, but these are already important hints. Here we find the beginnings of answers to questions about how an ecclesially located theological interpretation might take the biblical text seriously without neglecting or prioritizing historical criticism. And here we find evidence that Wesley's theological interpretation, and our own, need not be "uncritical."

# Afterword

Despite good intentions and sometimes imaginative initiatives, the disciplines of theology and biblical studies have drifted apart. Today, they are hardly on speaking terms, not so much because of deep-seated enmity but because, for all practical purposes, they speak different languages. Within theological schools, although the departments of biblical studies and theological studies may share a relationship of mutual respect, the assumptions and practices that they represent are constitutive of different epistemic communities, each regulated by standards of excellence and aims that overlap very little. Indeed, it is not hard to find scholars trained according to the accredited standards of the one discipline patrolling against the presumed naive or colonizing efforts of the other.

How best to model the relation of Scripture to theology? Johann Philipp Gabler inspired the now pervasive answer more than two hundred years ago when he sketched a three-stage process by which one might move from biblical studies to theology: (1) linguistic and historical analysis of biblical texts; (2) identification of ideas common among the biblical writers; and (3) articulation of the Bible's timeless and universal principles. A hermeneutical commitment to observer neutrality (as opposed to an interpreter guided by theological commitments), together with an unswerving focus on the historical rootedness of the text, the historicity of events to which the text bears witness, and the historical gap separating text and reader, emerged as key coordinates in the work of interpretation. Consequently, biblical studies was denuded of inherent religious interests, and biblical scholars increasingly saw themselves as philologists and historians rather than as theologians. At most, their job would be to describe the theological content or perspective of the biblical materials, leaving to others the constructive and prescriptive theological tasks. Unfortunately, theologians and ethicists have been left to sift through stacks and stacks of exegetical hay in search of that rare needle of theological consequence.

An alternative approach recasts biblical studies as an inherently theological enterprise, one that resists the common division of labor that identifies one group (theologians) for its interest in speaking of God in the present tense while insisting that another group (biblical scholars) confine itself to speaking of God only in the past tense. The predominant image would no longer be "building a bridge" from biblical scholarship to ecclesial communities, nor "crossing the bridge" from text to sermon, nor "passing the baton in a relay race" from exegesis to biblical theology to systematic theology to ethics. Instead, biblical studies would self-consciously locate itself within the church, just as the church works out its identity and mission in the world. Other ways of engaging the biblical materials might continue, of course. Theological engagement with Scripture has no need to exclude other interpretive agendas, but only insists that reading the Bible theologically as Christian Scripture has its own inherently theological presumptions and protocols.

Few of us can claim anything more than novitiate status as theological interpreters. This is because the tradition built up from hundreds of years of biblical studies and our own training in exegetical method and practice have left us with sensibilities and interpretive habits foreign to theological interpretation. We naturally ask about historical context. Inquiry into whether we find the triune God in Mark's baptismal scene (1:9–11) seems an alien intrusion into serious biblical study. (Could the final redactor of the Gospel of Mark have anticipated the trinitarian debates of later centuries?) The reemergence of theological interpretation raises questions, and the preceding chapters have taken up only a few of them. Others remain, not the least of which has to do with the unity and diversity among the biblical materials, and by what criteria we might rule some readings of Scripture as better or worse, or even out of bounds. We need to give more attention to how we might learn from premodern exegetes (whose theological interests were typically more fully visible in their readings of Scripture than they are in our own) while not overlooking the gains made in the modern era (including questions about unity and diversity and problems resident in interpretive practices that effectively denude ancient texts of their antiquity). Most important, we need more exemplars of theological interpretation, together with patience as we experiment with what is for many of us a lost-but-newly-found practice.

More work needs to be done and more questions answered. Marks of this ongoing practice might include such assumptions and approaches as the following.

*Theological claims.* Theological engagement with Scripture revolves around two theological affirmations, one concerning the Bible, the other concerning the nature of the church. First, theological reading of Scripture takes as its starting point and central axis the theological claim that "the Bible is Scripture," a claim that draws attention to the origin, role, and aim of these texts in God's self-communication. It locates those who read the Bible as Scripture on a particular textual map, a location possessing its own assumptions, values, and norms for guiding and animating particular beliefs, dispositions, and practices constitutive of that people.

Second, concerning the church, theological engagement with Scripture takes seriously the claim that the church is "one." Consequently, the texts that constitute the Bible were traditioned, written, and preserved by the same people of God now faced with the task of appropriating and embodying its message; this is the same community that received this collection of texts as canon; and this is the very community to which these texts were and are addressed. That is, we locate "the meaning" of Scripture not in the distant past in a faraway land, but rather in the community of God's people—past, present, and future.

*Theological dispositions.* What might it mean to make sense of biblical texts? Modern exegesis has construed this question especially in terms of historical distance: how to span the chasm between our world and the strange world of the Bible. The hermeneutical task requires the scholar to enter that world like a pioneer, subdue the text, and bring back its meaning, now transformed and conceptually translated for our world. Theological interpretation focuses elsewhere, on the degree to which we share (or refuse) the theological vision of the biblical text and in terms of our disposition to "stand under" (or to defy) the Scriptures. That is, theological interpretation locates our practices of engaging with Scripture in relation to our commitments to live faithfully before the God to whom the Scriptures witness. Therefore, dispositions and practices such as attention, acceptance, devotion, and trust characterize theological interpretation.

This does not mean that reading the Bible theologically requires apathy concerning historical questions, as though the last two centuries of a biblical scholarship characterized by its orientation toward historical issues were unimportant or unnecessary. Quite the contrary, we have learned that attention to historical questions may serve to shield the text from domestication or objectification by the reader, by working to allow the text its own voice from within its own sociocultural horizons. We recognize that these texts are present to us as cultural products that draw on, actualize, propagate, and/or undermine the contexts within which they were generated. Accordingly, the aim of historical work would shift from the discovery of meaning embedded in or behind the text to hearing the robust voice of the text as a subject (rather than an object) in theological discourse.

*Theological horizons*. For theological work, the horizons of interpretation of these texts include the particularity of the ecclesial community. This means that the measure of validity for Christian theological interpretation cannot be taken apart from the great creeds of the church, a concern with the Rule of Faith, and the history of Christian interpretation and its embodiment in Christian lives and communities. This does not mean that the now traditional categories of systematic theology must govern the meaning of these texts, much less that the aim of theological interpretation would be to generate and organize faith claims. Theological reading is concerned, rather, with putting into play (or facilitating the performance of) the witness of Scripture. We do not invite the text into a transformation of its original meaning into a new application geared toward our thought forms; rather, the text invites us into a transformation of allegiances and commitments that will manifest itself in Scripture-shaped practices. What might it mean to work theologically *with the text* as opposed, say, to doing theology *on the basis of the text*?

*Theological method*. What of "method"? Given the modern fascination with technique, we should recognize that no particular method can guarantee a faithful reading of the Bible as Scripture. Nevertheless, some methods are more hospitable to theological reading than others. In addition to approaches that situate the voice of Scripture sociohistorically, of special interest in theological interpretation are modes of analysis that take seriously the generally narrative content of Scripture; the theological unity of Scripture, which takes its point of departure from the character and purpose of the God of Israel and of Jesus Christ, and which gives rise to the unity of Scripture as the narrative of that purpose being worked out in the cosmos; and the final form and canonical location of the biblical texts.

# Bibliography

Abraham, William J. *Canon and Criterion in Christian Theology: From the Fathers to Feminism.* Oxford: Oxford University Press, 1998.

Abrams, M. H. *The Mirror and the Lamp: Romantic Theory and the Critical Tradition.* New York: Oxford University Press, 1953.

Adams, Hazard, ed. *Critical Theory since Plato.* Rev. ed. Fort Worth: Harcourt Brace Jovanovich, 1992.

Archer, Kenneth J. *A Pentecostal Hermeneutic for the Twenty-First Century: Spirit, Scripture and Community.* JPTSup 28. London: T&T Clark, 2004.

———. "Pentecostal Hermeneutics: Retrospect and Prospect." *JPT* 8 (1996): 63–81.

Autry, Arden C. "Dimensions of Hermeneutics in Pentecostal Focus." *JPT* 3 (1993): 29–50.

Baker, Robert O. "Pentecostal Bible Reading: Toward a Model of Reading for the Formation of Christian Affections." *JPT* 7 (1995): 34–48.

Barrett, C. K. *A Critical and Exegetical Commentary on the Acts of the Apostles.* Vol. 3. ICC. Edinburgh: T&T Clark, 1994.

Barth, Karl. "The Strange New World within the Bible." In *The Word of God and the Word of Man*, translated by Douglas Horton, 28–50. Gloucester, MA: Peter Smith, 1978.

Barton, John. *The Nature of Biblical Criticism*. Louisville: Westminster John Knox, 2007.

Berger, Klaus. *Formgeschichte des Neuen Testaments*. Heidelberg: Quelle & Meyer, 1984.

———. "Rhetorical Criticism, New Form Criticism, and New Testament Hermeneutics." In *Rhetoric and the New Testament: Essays from the 1992 Heidelberg Conference*, edited by Stanley E. Porter and Thomas H. Olbricht, 390–96. JSNTSup 90. Sheffield: Sheffield Academic Press, 1993.

Berger, Peter L., and Thomas Luckmann. *The Social Construction of Reality: A Treatise in the Sociology of Knowledge*. New York: Doubleday, 1966.

Blanke, Olaf, et al. "Linking Out-of-Body Experience and Self Processing to Mental Own-Body Imagery at the Temporoparietal Junction." *Journal of Neuroscience* 25, no. 3 (2005): 550–57.

———. "Out-of-Body Experience and Autoscopy of Neurological Origin." *Brain* 127 (2004): 243–58.

Bockmuehl, Markus. "Bible versus Theology: Is 'Theological Interpretation' the Answer?" *Nova et Vetera*, forthcoming.

———. "The Case against New England Clam Chowder and Other Questions about 'Theological Interpretation.'" Paper presented at the Annual Meeting of the Society of Biblical Literature, Boston, November 21–25, 2008.

———. *Seeing the Word: Refocusing New Testament Study*. STI. Grand Rapids: Baker Academic, 2006.

Bruce, F. F. *The Book of Acts*. Rev. ed. NICNT. Grand Rapids: Eerdmans, 1988.

Bultmann, Rudolf. "New Testament and Mythology: The Mythological Element in the Message of the New Testament and the Problem of Its Re-interpretation." In *Kerygma and Myth: A Theological Debate*, by Rudolf Bultmann et al., edited by Hans Werner Bartsch, 1–44. New York: Harper & Row, 1961.

Burnett, Richard E. *Karl Barth's Theological Exegesis: The Hermeneutical Principles of the* Römerbrief *Period*. Grand Rapids: Eerdmans, 2004.

Bynum, Caroline Walker. *The Resurrection of the Body in Western Christianity, 200–1336*. Lectures on the History of Religions n.s. 15. New York: Columbia University Press, 1995.

Cadbury, Henry J. "Note VII: The Hellenists." In *The Beginnings of Christianity*, Part 1: *The Acts of the Apostles*. Vol. 5, *Additional Notes to the Commentary*, edited by Kirsopp Lake and Henry J. Cadbury, 59–74. Grand Rapids: Baker, 1933.

Callen, Barry, and Richard P. Thompson, eds. *Reading the Bible in Wesleyan Ways: Some Constructive Proposals*. Kansas City, MO: Beacon Hill, 2004.

Cargal, Timothy B. *Restoring the Diaspora: Discursive Structure and Purpose in the Epistle of James*. SBLDS 144. Atlanta: Scholars Press, 1993.

Clark, Elizabeth A. *History, Theory, Text: Historians and the Linguistic Turn*. Cambridge, MA: Harvard University Press, 2004.

Clark, Timothy. "Recent Eastern Orthodox Interpretation of the New Testament." *CBR* 5 (2007): 322–40.

Cohen, Robin. *Global Diasporas: An Introduction*. Global Diasporas. Seattle: University of Washington Press, 1997.

Collins, John N. *Diakonia: Re-interpreting the Ancient Sources*. New York: Oxford University Press, 1990.

Conzelmann, Hans. *Acts of the Apostles*. Hermeneia. Philadelphia: Fortress, 1987.

Dunn, James D. G. *Christianity in the Making*. Vol. 1, *Jesus Remembered*. Grand Rapids: Eerdmans, 2003.

Duranti, Alessandro. *Linguistic Anthropology*. Cambridge Textbooks in Linguistics. Cambridge: Cambridge University Press, 1997.

Eco, Umberto. *The Limits of Interpretation*. Advances in Semiotics. Bloomington: Indiana University Press, 1990.

———. *The Role of the Reader: Explorations in the Semiotics of Texts*. Advances in Semiotics. Bloomington: Indiana University Press, 1979.

Eco, Umberto, with Richard Rorty, Jonathan Culler, and Christine Brooke-Rose. *Interpretation and Overinterpretation*. Edited by Stefan Collini. Cambridge: Cambridge University Press, 1992.

Feinberg, Todd E. *Altered Egos: How the Brain Creates the Self.* Oxford: Oxford University Press, 2001.

Ferguson, Duncan S. "John Wesley on Scripture: The Hermeneutics of Pietism." *Methodist History* 22 (1984): 234–45.

Finger, Reta Halteman. *Of Widows and Meals: Communal Meals in the Book of Acts*. Grand Rapids: Eerdmans, 2007.

Fitzmyer, Joseph A. *The Acts of the Apostles: A New Translation with Introduction and Commentary*. AB 31. New York: Doubleday, 1998.

Flanagan, Owen. *The Problem of the Soul: Two Visions of Mind and How to Reconcile Them*. New York: Basic Books, 2002.

Foakes-Jackson, F. J. *The Acts of the Apostles*. MNTC. London: Hodder & Stoughton, 1931.

Fowl, Stephen E. Introduction to *The Theological Interpretation of Scripture: Classic and Contemporary Readings*, edited by Stephen E. Fowl, xii–xxx. Blackwell Readings in Modern Theology. Cambridge, MA: Blackwell, 1997.

———. *Theological Interpretation of Scripture*. Cascade Companions. Eugene, OR: Cascade Books, 2009.

Fox, Michael V. "Bible Scholarship and Faith-Based Study: My View." SBL Forum. http://sbl-site.org/publications/article.aspx ?articleId=490.

Gaertner, Jan Felix, ed. *Writing Exile: The Discourse of Displacement in Greco-Roman Antiquity and Beyond*. Mnemosyne: Bibliotheca Classica Batava Supplementum 83. Leiden: Brill, 2007.

Green, Garrett. *Imagining God: Theology and the Religious Imagination*. Grand Rapids: Eerdmans, 1989.

———. *Theology, Hermeneutics, and Imagination: The Crisis of Interpretation at the End of Modernity*. Cambridge: Cambridge University Press, 2000.

Green, Joel B. *Body, Soul, and Human Life: The Nature of Humanity in the Bible*. STI. Grand Rapids: Baker Academic, 2008.

———, ed. *Hearing the New Testament: Strategies for Interpretation*. 2nd ed. Grand Rapids: Eerdmans, 2010.

———. "'In Our Own Languages': Pentecost, Babel, and the Shaping of Christian Community in Acts 2:1–13." In *The Word Leaps the Gap: Essays on Scripture and Theology in Honor of Richard B. Hays*, edited by J. Ross Wagner, C. Kavin Rowe, and A. Katherine Grieb, 198–213. Grand Rapids: Eerdmans, 2008.

———. "Modernity, History, and the Theological Interpretation of the Bible." *SJT* 54 (2001): 308–29.

———. "Neglecting Widows and Serving the Word? Acts 6:1–7 as a Test Case for a Missional Hermeneutic." In *Jesus Christ, Lord and Savior*, edited by Jon Laansma, Grant Osborne, and Ray Van Neste. Carlisle, UK: Paternoster; Eugene, OR: Wipf & Stock, forthcoming.

———. *1 Peter*. THNTC. Grand Rapids: Eerdmans, 2007.

———. *Reading Scripture as Wesleyans*. Nashville: Abingdon, 2010.

———. "Reading the Bible as Wesleyans." *WTJ* 33 (1998): 116–29.

———. *Seized by Truth: Reading the Bible as Scripture*. Nashville: Abingdon, 2007.

———. "What about . . . ? Three Exegetical Forays into the Body-Soul Discussion." *CTR* n.s. 7 (2010): 3–18.

Greenblatt, Stephen. "Culture." In *Critical Terms for Literary Study*, edited by Frank Lentricchia and Thomas McLaughlin, 225–32. Chicago: University of Chicago Press, 1990.

Grenz, Stanley J. *The Social God and the Relational Self: A Trinitarian Theology of the Imago Dei*. Matrix of Christian Theology. Louisville: Westminster John Knox, 2001.

Haenchen, Ernst. *The Acts of the Apostles*. Translated by Bernard Noble and Gerald Shinn. Oxford: Blackwell, 1971.

Haskell, Thomas L. "Objectivity Is Not Neutrality: Rhetoric versus Practice in Peter Novick's *That Noble Dream*." In *Objectivity Is Not Neutrality: Explanatory Schemes in History*, 145–73. Baltimore: Johns Hopkins University Press, 1998.

Hendel, Ronald S. "Farewell to SBL: Faith and Reason in Biblical Studies." *Biblical Archaeology Review* 36, no. 4 (July/August 2010): 28–29.

Hengel, Martin. "Between Jesus and Paul: The 'Hellenists,' the 'Seven' and Stephen." In *Between Jesus and Paul: Studies in the*

*Earliest History of Christianity*, translated by John Bowden, 1–29. Philadelphia: Fortress, 1983.

Heringer, Seth. "The Practice of Theological Commentary." *JTI* 4 (2010): 127–37.

Hill, Craig C. *Hellenists and Hebrews: Reappraising Division within the Earliest Church*. Minneapolis: Fortress, 1992.

Hirstein, William. *Brain Fiction: Self-Deception and the Riddle of Confabulation*. Cambridge, MA: MIT Press, 2005.

Iser, Wolfgang. *The Implied Reader: Patterns of Communication in Prose Fiction from Bunyan to Beckett*. Baltimore: Johns Hopkins University Press, 1974.

Israel, Richard D., Daniel E. Albrecht, and Randal G. McNally. "Pentecostals and Hermeneutics: Texts, Rituals and Community." *Pneuma* 15 (1993): 137–61.

Jenson, Robert W. "The Religious Power of Scripture." *SJT* 52 (1999): 89–105.

Johns, Jackie David, and Cheryl Bridges Johns. "Yielding to the Spirit: A Pentecostal Approach to Group Bible Study." *JPT* 1 (1992): 109–34.

Johnson, Luke Timothy. *Brother of Jesus, Friend of God: Studies in the Letter of James*. Grand Rapids: Eerdmans, 2004.

———. *The Letter of James: A New Translation with Introduction and Commentary*. AB 37A. New York: Doubleday, 1995.

Johnson, Mark. *The Body in the Mind: The Bodily Basis of Meaning, Imagination, and Reason*. Chicago: University of Chicago Press, 1987.

Koch, Christof. *The Quest for Consciousness: A Neurobiological Approach*. Englewood, CO: Roberts, 2004.

Koskie, Steven J. "Reading the Way to Heaven: A Wesleyan Theological Hermeneutic of Scripture." PhD diss., London School of Theology–Brunel University, 2010.

Larsen, Kasper Bro. "Narrative Docetism: Christology and Storytelling in the Gospel of John." In *The Gospel of John and Christian Theology*, edited by Richard Bauckham and Carl Mosser, 346–55. Grand Rapids: Eerdmans, 2008.

Laws, Sophie. *A Commentary on the Epistle of James*. HNTC. San Francisco: Harper & Row, 1980.

Lienhard, Joseph T. "Acts 6:1–6: A Redactional View." *CBQ* 37 (1975): 228–36.

Lincoln, Andrew T. "The Lazarus Story: A Literary Perspective." In *The Gospel of John and Christian Theology*, edited by Richard Bauckham and Carl Mosser, 211–32. Grand Rapids: Eerdmans, 2008.

Lindbeck, George A. *The Nature of Doctrine: Religion and Theology in a Postliberal Age*. Philadelphia: Westminster, 1984.

Lindsell, Harold. *The Battle for the Bible*. Grand Rapids: Zondervan, 1976.

Longenecker, Richard N. "The Foundational Conviction of New Testament Christology: The Obedience/Faithfulness/Sonship of Christ." In *Jesus of Nazareth, Lord and Christ: Essays on the Historical Jesus and New Testament Christology*, edited by Joel B. Green and Max Turner, 473–88. Grand Rapids: Eerdmans, 1994.

Lowenthal, David. *The Past Is a Foreign Country*. Cambridge: Cambridge University Press, 1985.

Lüdemann, Gerd. *Early Christianity according to the Traditions in Acts: A Commentary*, translated by John Bowden. Minneapolis: Fortress, 1989.

MacDonald, Paul S. *History of the Concept of Mind: Speculation about Soul, Mind and Spirit from Homer to Hume*. Aldershot, UK: Ashgate, 2003.

McCartney, Dan G. *James*. BECNT. Grand Rapids: Baker Academic, 2009.

McClendon, James Wm., Jr. *Systematic Theology*. Vol. 1, *Ethics*. Nashville: Abingdon, 1986.

McGrath, Alister E. *The Genesis of Doctrine: A Study in the Foundation of Doctrinal Criticism*. Grand Rapids: Eerdmans, 1990.

McGuckin, John Anthony, ed. *We Believe in One Lord Jesus Christ*. Ancient Christian Doctrine 2. Downers Grove, IL: IVP Academic, 2009.

McIntire, C. T. "Transcending Dichotomies in History and Religion." *History and Theory* 45 (2006): 80–92.

Meier, John P. *A Marginal Jew: Rethinking the Historical Jesus*. Vol. 1, *The Roots of the Problem and the Person*. ABRL. New York: Doubleday, 1991.

Middleton, J. Richard. *The Liberating Image: The* Imago Dei *in Genesis 1.* Grand Rapids: Brazos, 2005.

Morgan, Robert, with John Barton. *Biblical Interpretation.* Oxford Bible Series. Oxford: Oxford University Press, 1988.

Mullen, Wilbur H. "John Wesley's Method of Biblical Interpretation." *Religion in Life* 47 (1978): 99–108.

Novick, Peter. *The Noble Dream: The "Objectivity Question" and the American Historical Profession.* Ideas in Context. Cambridge: Cambridge University Press, 1988.

O'Keefe, John J., and R. R. Reno. *Sanctified Vision: An Introduction to Early Christian Interpretation of the Bible.* Baltimore: Johns Hopkins University Press, 2005.

Paden, William E. *Religious Worlds: The Comparative Study of Religion.* Boston: Beacon, 1994.

Parsons, Mikeal. *Acts.* Paideia. Grand Rapids: Baker Academic, 2008.

Pelikan, Jaroslav. *Acts.* BTCB. Grand Rapids: Brazos, 2005.

Penner, Todd C. *The Epistle of James and Eschatology: Re-reading an Ancient Christian Letter.* JSNTSup 121. Sheffield: Sheffield Academic Press, 1996.

Pervo, Richard I. *Acts: A Commentary.* Hermeneia. Minneapolis: Fortress, 2009.

———. *Dating Acts: Between the Evangelists and the Apologists.* Santa Rosa, CA: Polebridge, 2006.

Pesch, Rudolf. *Die Apostelgeschichte.* Vol. 1. EKKNT 5. Zürich: Benziger; Neukirchen-Vluyn: Neukirchener Verlag, 1986.

Phelan, James. *Narrative as Rhetoric: Technique, Audiences, Ethics, Ideology.* Columbus: Ohio State University Press, 1996.

Philo. *Philo.* 10 vols. Translated by F. H. Colson and G. H. Whitaker. Loeb Classical Library. Cambridge, MA: Harvard University Press, 1926–62.

Polhill, John B. *Acts.* NAC. Nashville: Broadman, 1992.

Powell, Mark Allan. *What Is Narrative Criticism?* GBS. Minneapolis: Fortress, 1990.

Rabinowitz, Peter J. "Reader-Response Theory and Criticism." In *The Johns Hopkins Guide to Literary Theory and Criticism,* edited by Michael Groden and Martin Kreiswirth, 606–9. Baltimore: Johns Hopkins University Press, 1994.

Rackham, Richard Belward. *The Acts of the Apostles: An Exposition*. London: Methuen, 1906.

Rae, Murray. *History and Hermeneutics*. London: T&T Clark, 2005.

Räisänen, Heikki. *Beyond New Testament Theology: A Story and a Programme*. 2nd ed. London: SCM, 2000.

Robinson, T. M. "The Defining Features of Mind-Body Dualism in the Writings of Plato." In *Psyche and Soma: Physicians and Metaphysicians on the Mind-Body Problem from Antiquity to Enlightenment*, edited by John P. Wright and Paul Potter, 37–55. Oxford: Oxford University Press, 2000.

Sahlins, Marshall. *Stone Age Economics*. London: Routledge, 1972.

Sanders, E. P. *Jesus and Judaism*. London: SCM, 1985.

Schaff, Philip. *The Creeds of Christendom: With a History and Critical Notes*. Revised by Davis S. Schaff. 6th ed. 3 vols. Grand Rapids: Baker, 1983 (1931).

Schleiermacher, Friedrich. *The Christian Faith*. Philadelphia: Fortress, 1928.

Schneider, Gerhard. *Die Apostelgeschichte*. Vol. 1. HTKNT 5. Freiburg: Herder, 1980.

Schorske, Carl E. *Thinking with History: Explorations in the Passage to Modernism*. Princeton, NJ: Princeton University Press, 1998.

Schweizer, Eduard, et al. "ψυχή κτλ." *TDNT* 9:608–66.

Scroggs, Robin. "John Wesley as Biblical Scholar." *JBR* 28 (1960): 415–22.

Seim, Turid Karlsen. *The Double Message: Patterns of Gender in Luke and Acts*. Nashville: Abingdon, 1994.

Seitz, Aaron R., Jose E. Nanez, Steven R. Holloway, Shinichi Koyama, and Takeo Watanabe. "Seeing What Is Not There Shows the Costs of Perceptual Learning." *Proceedings of the National Academy of Sciences* 102, no. 25 (2005): 9080–85.

Seymour-Smith, Charlotte. *Macmillan Dictionary of Anthropology*. London: Macmillan, 1986.

Shults, F. LeRon. *Christology and Science*. Grand Rapids: Eerdmans, 2008.

Siegel, Daniel J. *The Mindful Brain: Reflection and Attunement in the Cultivation of Well-Being*. New York: Norton, 2007.

Smith, Steven G. "Historical Meaningfulness in Shared Action." *History and Theory* 48 (2009): 1–19.

Smith-Christopher, Daniel L. *A Biblical Theology of Exile*. OBT. Minneapolis: Fortress, 2002.

Sorabji, Richard. *Self: Ancient and Modern Insights about Individuality, Life, and Death*. Chicago: University of Chicago Press, 2006.

Spencer, F. Scott. "Neglected Widows in Acts 6:1–7." *CBQ* 56 (1994): 715–33.

Spohn, William C. *Go and Do Likewise: Jesus and Ethics*. New York: Continuum, 2000.

Steenberg, M. C. *Of God and Man: Theology as Anthropology from Irenaeus to Athanasius*. London: T&T Clark, 2009.

Steinmetz, David C. "The Superiority of Pre-critical Exegesis." *ThTo* 37, no. 1 (1980): 27–38.

Stock, Brian. *Listening for the Text: On the Uses of the Past*. Parallax Re-Visions of Culture and Society. Baltimore: Johns Hopkins University Press, 1990.

Stott, John R. W. *Between Two Worlds: The Challenge of Preaching Today*. Grand Rapids: Eerdmans, 1982.

Stronstad, Roger. "Trends in Pentecostal Hermeneutics." *Paraclete* 22, no. 3 (1998): 1–12.

Thomas, John Christopher. "Reading the Bible from within Our Traditions: A Pentecostal Hermeneutic as Test Case." In *Between Two Horizons: Spanning New Testament Studies and Systematic Theology*, edited by Joel B. Green and Max Turner, 108–22. Grand Rapids: Eerdmans, 2000.

Torrance, Alan. "The Lazarus Narrative, Theological History, and Historical Probability." In *The Gospel of John and Christian Theology*, edited by Richard Bauckham and Carl Mosser, 245–62. Grand Rapids: Eerdmans, 2008.

Towner, W. Sibley. "Clones of God: Genesis 1:26–28 and the Image of God in the Hebrew Bible." *Int* 59 (2005): 341–56.

Treier, Daniel J. *Introducing Theological Interpretation of Scripture: Recovering a Christian Practice.* Grand Rapids: Baker Academic, 2008.

Troeltsch, Ernst. "Historical and Dogmatic Method in Theology." In *Religion in History*, edited by James Luther Adams and Walter F. Bense, 11–32. Edinburgh: T&T Clark, 1991.

Turner, George A. "John Wesley as an Interpreter of Scripture." In *Inspiration and Interpretation*, edited by John F. Walvoord, 156–78. Grand Rapids: Eerdmans, 1957.

Turner, Mark. *The Literary Mind: The Origins of Thought and Language.* Oxford: Oxford University Press, 1996.

Tyson, Joseph B. "Acts 6:1–7 and Dietary Regulations in Early Christianity." *PRSt* 10 (1983): 145–61.

Vanhoozer, Kevin J., ed. *Dictionary for Theological Interpretation of the Bible.* Grand Rapids: Baker Academic, 2005.

Vann, Richard T., Nancy Partner, Ewa Domanska, and F. R. Ankersmit. "Hayden White: Twenty-Five Years On." *History and Theory* 37 (1998): 143–93.

von Staden, Heinrich. "Body, Soul, and Nerves: Epicurus, Herophilus, Erasistratus, the Stoics, and Galen." In *Psyche and Soma: Physicians and Metaphysicians on the Mind-Body Problem from Antiquity to Enlightenment*, edited by John P. Wright and Paul Potter, 79–116. Oxford: Oxford University Press, 2000.

Ware, Kallistos. "The Soul in Greek Christianity." In *From Soul to Self*, edited by M. James C. Crabbe, 49–69. London: Routledge, 1999.

Wenk, Matthias. *Community-Forming Power: The Socio-Ethical Role of the Spirit in Luke-Acts.* JPTSup 19. Sheffield: Sheffield Academic Press, 2000.

Wesley, John. *Explanatory Notes upon the New Testament.* London: Epworth, 1976 (1754).

———. *The Works of John Wesley.* 14 vols. 3rd ed. Edited by Thomas Jackson. Grand Rapids: Baker, 1979 [1872].

White, Hayden. *The Content of the Form: Narrative Discourse and Historical Representation.* Baltimore: Johns Hopkins University Press, 1987.

Willis, Thomas. *The Anatomy of the Brain and Nerves*. Translated by Samuel Pordage. Edited by William Feindel. Classics of Medicine Library. Birmingham, UK: McGill-Queens University Press, 1978 (1681).

Wood, Charles M. *The Formation of Christian Understanding: An Essay in Theological Hermeneutics*. Philadelphia: Westminster, 1981.

Work, Telford. *Deuteronomy*. BTCB. Grand Rapids: Brazos, 2009.

Wrede, William. "The Task and Methods of 'New Testament Theology.'" In *The Nature of New Testament Theology: The Contribution of William Wrede and Adolf Schlatter*, edited and translated by Robert Morgan, 68–116. SBT s.s. 25. Naperville, IL: Allenson, 1973.

Young, Kay, and Jeffrey L. Saver. "The Neurology of Narrative." *SubStance* 30 (2001): 72–84.

Zaleski, Carol. *The Life of the World to Come: Near-Death Experience and Christian Hope*. New York: Oxford University Press, 1996.

# Scripture Index

# Modern Author Index

# Subject Index